THE PEOPLE OF THE GRAMPIAN HIGHLANDS
1600 - 1699

By
David Dobson

CLEARFIELD

Copyright © 2023
by David Dobson
All Rights Reserved

Published for Clearfield Company by
Genealogical Publishing Company
Baltimore, Maryland
2023

ISBN: 9780806359595

INTRODUCTION

The Grampian Highlands lie in North East Scotland and stretch from Aberdeenshire, through Kincardineshire, the Braes of Angus, to Eastern Perthshire. In the seventeenth century the majority of the population were Gaelic speaking. The region sported only a handful of small burghs, such as Kincardine O'Neill or Fettercairn, with most people dispersed throughout the region, mainly in fermtouns or isolated crofts, and employed in agriculture, notably cattle rearing.

The Grampian Highlands were mostly controlled by landowners such as the Earl of Aboyne or the Earl of Airlie, or heads of families or clans such as Forbes, Gordon, Farquharson, Burnett, Irvine, Douglas, Lindsay, Carnegie, Ogilvie, Spalding, Stewart, and Robertson. These families were generally Royalist and supporters of the House of Stuart, notably in the Jacobite Wars of 1689, 1715, and 1745.

Most seventeenth-century Highlanders, however, were Protestants (Presbyterian and Episcopalian), with a few Roman Catholics in remote glens, such as around Braemar. Emigration from the Grampian Highlands did not occur until the early eighteenth century, apart from prisoners of war banished to the Plantations.

David Dobson

Dundee, 2023

Birse Castle, view from the north-east. Forest of Birse, Aberdeenshire

Mar Castle, view from the south-west. South of old town Aberdeen

Craighall of Clan Rattray, Blairgowrie, Perth and Kinross

Dunkeld Cathedral, Dunkeld, Perth and Kinross

Grandtully Castle, view from the south-west. Grandtully, Perth and Kinross

Eicho Castle, view from the south-east. Southeast of Perth

Scene in the Grampians: stormy

Scene in the Grampians: fair weather

Airlie gravestone, Airlie, Angus

PEOPLE OF THE GRAMPIAN HIGHLANDS, 1600-1699

ABERCROMBIE, FRANCIS, of Fetterneir, Aberdeenshire, a deed in 1696.

ABERCROMBIE, ROBERT, a servant in the parish of Crathie, Aberdeenshire, in 1696. [PT]

ADAM, BEATRIX, in Meikle Davie, Glen Isla, Angus, testament, 1659, Comm. Brechin. [NRS]

ADAM, AGNES, in the Kirkton of Kingoldrum, Angus, testament, 1634, Comm. Brechin. [NRS]

ADAM, BEATRIX, in Meikle Davie, Glen Isla, Angus, testament, 1659, Comm. Brechin. [NRS]

ADAM, GEORGE, in Lethnott-Lochlee, Angus, 1691. [NRS.E69.11.1]

ADAM, GEORGE, born 1629, a tenant, husband of Christian Henderson, died in April 1695. [Airlie gravestone, Angus]

ADAM, JAMES, born 1628, graduated MA from St Andrews University in 1648, minister of Cortachy, Angus, from 1659 to 1678, and from 1691 to his death in 1692, husband of Christian Straton, parents of Katherine and Matilda, in Cortachy, around 1710; a sasine, testament, 1695, Comm. Brechin. [NRS.RS35.12.238][F.5.280]

ADAM, JOHN, and his wife Janet Nicoll, in Meikle Derry, Glen Isla, Angus, testament, 1612, Comm. Brechin. [NRS],

ADAM, JOHN, of Milntoun of Blacklunans, Angus, husband of Janet Cudbert, a sasine, 1648. [NRS.RS34.2.III.8].

ADAM, JOHN, born 1625, husband of Isobel Gibbon in Clinto, died -8 December 1678. [Airlie gravestone, Angus]

ADAM, THOMAS, in Lintrathen, Angus, 1691. [NRS.E69.11.1]

ADAMSON, ANNA, at the Mill of Gellen in the parish of Coull, Aberdeenshire, 1696. [PT]

ADAMSON. JOHN, in Claecleugh, Glen Clova, Angus, in 1662. [RGS.XI.178]

ADAMSON, JOHN, in Alyth, Perthshire, in 1691. [Hearth Tax Roll] [NRS.E69.19.1]

ADAMSON, MARGARET, spouse to John Adeson in Crag Ruiff, Cortachy, Angus, testament, 1611, Comm. Brechin. [NRS]

ADAMSON, THOMAS, in Cortachy and Clova, Angus, 1691. [NRS.E69.11.1]

ADESON, JOHN, in Craigruiff, Cortachy, Angus, husband of Margaret Adamson, testament, 1611, Comm. Brechin. [NRS]

AIKENHEAD, JOHN, born 1604, died in 1672, [Fettercairn gravestone, Kincardineshire]

AITKEN, DAVID, schoolmaster at Strathcathro, Angus, 1690. [SHS.4.2]

AITKEN, ROBERT, from Kincardineshire, a soldier guarding the Scottish Regalia then in Dunottar Castle from Cromwell's Army from 1651-1652. [DR]

ALEXANDER, ALEXANDER, and his wife Isobel Fotheringham, in Capo, Strathcathro, Angus, testament, 1628, Comm. Brechin. [NRS]

ALEXANDER, ALEXANDER, in Strathcathro, Angus, testament, 1661, Comm. Brechin. [NRS]

ALEXANDER, JOHN, and his wife Janet Clark, in Easter Innerarity, Glen Isla, Angus, testament, 1610, Comm. Brechin. [NRS]

ALEXANDER, WILLIAM, in Lintrathen, Angus, 1691. [NRS.E69.11.1]

ANDERSON, CHRISTINE, in the barony of Glenisla, Angus, in 1663. [RGS.XI.464]

ALEXANDER, GEORGE, a waulker, with his wife, in Milltown of Glen Buchat, Aberdeenshire. [1696 Poll Tax]

ALEXANDER, JANET, spouse to John Wison in Bellitie, Glen Isla, Angus, testament, 1625, Comm. Brechin. [NRS]

ALEXANDER, JANET, spouse to John Nicoll in Cannock, Glen Isla, Angus, testament in 1629, Comm. Brechin. [NRS]

ALEXANDER, JOHN, son of the late David Alexander in Tilliquhomrie, parish of Strachan, Kincardineshire, testament, 1597, Comm. Brechin. [NRS]

ALEXANDER, JOHN, and his spouse Janet Clark in Easter Inverarity, Glen Isla, Angus, testament in 1610, Comm. Brechin. [NRS]

ALEXANDER, JOHN, in Alehousehill, Brechin, Angus, testament, 1612, Comm. Brechin. [NRS]

ALEXANDER, JOHN, servant to John Mitchell, a militiaman in Lintrathen, Angus, 1643. [NRS.GD16.50.17.4]

ALEXANDER, JOHN, a mariner from Careston, Angus, died at sea, probate 1684, PCC. [TNA]

ALEXANDER, VIOLET, spouse to Alexander Wilson in Cambok, Glen Isla, Angus, a testament, 1581, Comm. Brechin. [NRS]

ALEXANDER, WILLIAM, in Kirkhillocks, Glen Isla, Angus, husband of Agnes Jamie or Bruce, testament, 1625, Comm. Brechin. [NRS]

ALGO, JAMES, servant of Donald Findlay tenant in Milton of Inchmarn, Glen Muick, Aberdeenshire, in 1696. [PT]

ALLAN, ANDREW, MA, minister of Clova, Angus, from 1615 to 1622. [F.5.278]

ALLAN, DAVID, in Rotwell, Cortachy, Angus, testament, 1651, Comm. Brechin. [NRS]

ALLAN, GILBERT, in Middle Todd, a militiaman in Lintrathen, Angus, 1643. [NRS.GD16.50.17.4]

ALLAN, JOHN, in Ficheill, Angus, testament,1637, husband of Christian Ogilvie, testament, 1629, Comm. Brechin. [NRS]

ALLAN, JOHN, born 1586, died 1631, his wife Isobel Thomson, born 1579, died 1641. [Airlie gravestone, Angus]

ALLAN, JOHN, a militiaman in Balloh, Cortachy, Angus, 1643. [NRS.GD16.50.17.4]

ALLAN, THOMAS, in Westerton of Strathcathro, Angus, testament, 1693, Comm. Brechin. [NRS]

ALLAN, WILLIAM, and his spouse Agnes Brew, in New Crage, Glen Isla, Perthshire, testament, 1688, Comm. Brechin. [NRS]

ALLAN, WILLIAM, was granted the lands of Fettercairn, Kincardineshire, on 20 April 1692. [NRS.SIG.1.355]

ALLANACH, DUNCAN, a sub-tenant in Invercauld in the parish of Kindrochit/Braemar, Aberdeenshire, in 1696. [PT]

ALLAND, WILLIAM, from Kincardineshire, a soldier guarding the Scottish Regalia then in Dunottar Castle from Cromwell's Army from 1651-1652. [DR]

ALSHUNDER, JEAN, spouse of John Grig a wright in Innermark, Glen Esk, Angus, sasines, 1643. [NRS.RS7.3.338; RS7.4.201/204]

AMBROSE, GEORGE, in Blairgowrie, Perthshire, in 1691. [Hearth Tax Roll] [NRS.E69.19.1]

ANDERSON, ARTHUR, in part of Candercraig, Tarland, Aberdeenshire, 1667. [AVR]

ANDERSON, CHRISTINA, in Glenmarkie, barony of Glen Isla, Angus, 1667. [RGS.XI.1105]

ANDERSON, DAVID, a militiaman at Craigila, Lintrathen, Angus, 1643. [NRS.GD16.50.17.4]

ANDERSON, DAVID, in Mill of Haugh, Strachan, Kincardineshire, testament, 1709, Comm. Brechin. [NRS]

ANDERSON, GILBERT, husband of Isobel Schireff, at the Waulkmill of Forbes, Aberdeenshire, a sasine, 25 May 1607. [NRS.RS6.48]

ANDERSON, JAMES, in Westerton, a militiaman in Lintrathen, Angus, 1643. [NRS.GD16.50.17.4]

ANDERSON, JAMES, in Edzell, Angus, 1691. [NRS.E69.11.1]

ANDERSON, JOHN, in Dubbiton, Fern, Angus, testament, 1596, Comm. Brechin. [NRS]

ANDERSON, JOHN, in Elrick, Glen Isla, Angus, husband of Margaret McNicoll, testament, 1610, Comm. Brechin. [NRS]

ANDERSON, JOHN, a militiaman in Lintrathen, Angus, 1643. [NRS.GD16.50.17.4]

ANDERSON, JOHN, a servant to James Wright and a militiaman at Campsie, Lintrathen, Angus, 1643. [NRS.GD16.50.17.4]

ANDERSON, JOHN, son of William Anderson sometime at the Kirk of Alford, Aberdeenshire, was apprenticed to Andrew Craighead in Aberdeen on 4 April 1661. [ACA]

ANDERSON, JOHN, in Migvie, Aberdeenshire, 1667. [AVR]

ANDERSON, JOHN, in Lintrathen, Angus, 1691. [NRS.E69.11.1]

ANDERSON, KATHERINE, spouse to Thomas Bruce in Cureford, parish of Navar, Angus, testament, 1611, Comm. Brechin. [NRS]

ANDERSON, THOMAS, in Edzell, Angus, 1691. [NRS.E69.11.1]

ANDERSON, THOMAS, in Alyth, Perthshire, in 1691. [Hearth Tax Roll] [NRS.E69.19.1]

ANDERSON, WILLIAM, servant to Lady Jean Douglas or Gordon in Glenbuchat, Aberdeenshire. [1696 Poll Tax]

ANDREW, CHRISTIAN, spouse to John MacNicoll in Easter Inverarity, Glen Isla, Angus, testament, 1610, Comm. Brechin. [NRS]

ANGUS, WILLIAM, a militiaman in Airlie, Angus, 1643. [NRS.GD16.50.17.4]

ANNAND, GILBERT, of the Earl of Airlie's Militia, Angus, 1670. [NRS.GD16.53.39]

ANNAND, JAMES, of Persie, Angus, a bond with his wife Elizabeth Ramsay, concerning her life rent, dated 16 July 1636. Witnesses were James Crichtoun of Ruthven, James Blair of Ardblair, James Ogilvy servant to Gilbert Ramsay, and Patrick Robertson a notary. [BC.219] [NRS.83]

ANSTRUTHER, PHILIP, of Major Burnett's Troop of Dragoons, from Aberdeenshire, was mustered at Stirling on 10 December 1692. [FBL.295]

ARBUTHNOT, JEAN, spouse to William Burnett in Heugh of Pitrodde, Strachan, Kincardineshire, testament, 1610, Comm. Brechin. [NRS]

ARCHIBALD, ANDREW, in Menmuir, Angus, 1691. [NRS.E69.11.1]

ARCHIBALD, JOHN in Lethnott-Lochlee, Angus, 1691. [NRS.E69.11.1]

ARCHIBALD, ANDREW, and his wife Isobel Smart, in Pitmudie, testament, 1656, Comm. Brechin. [NRS]

ARCHIBALD, CHARLES, a servant and a militiaman in Raverny, Lintrathen, Angus, 1643. [NRS.GD16.50.17.4]

ARCHIBALD, JOHN, in Cortachy and Clova, Angus, 1691. [NRS.E69.11.1]

ARRAT, JAMES, in Inverquharritie, Angus, husband of Isobel Crichton, a sasine, 1649. [NRS.RS34.III.324.411]

ARROT, WILLIAM, and his spouse Margaret Fullarton, in Grange of Airlie, Angus, testament, 1659, Comm. Brechin. [NRS]

ARROT, WILLIAM, of the Earl of Airlie's Militia, Angus, 1670. [NRS.GD16.53.39]

AUCHENLECK, GEORGE, from Kincardineshire, a soldier guarding the Scottish Regalia then in Dunottar Castle from Cromwell's Army from 1651-1652. [DR]

AUCHENLECK, JAMES, of the Earl of Airlie's Militia, Angus, 1670. [NRS.GD16.53.39]

AUCHTERLONIE, DAVID, minister at Fordoun, Kincardineshire, a sasine, 1662. [NRS.RS35.I.259]

AULD, DAVID, a tailor in Airlie, Angus, 1691. [NRS.E69.11.1]; 1643. [NRS.GD16.50.17.4]

AUSTIN, WILLIAM, born 1617, died 30 June 1685, husband of Isobel Gentleman. [Fettercairn gravestone, Kincardineshire]

BAILLIE, WILLIAM, in the Nethertoun of Melgund, Angus, husband of Anne Junking, a sasine 1673. [NRS.RS35.V.100]

BALFOUR, JOHN, a gardener in Fetteresso, Kincardineshire, husband of Christian Burnett, sasines, 1675. [NRS.RS35.VI.49/54]

BALVAIRD, JOHN, in Edzell, Angus, 1691. [NRS.E69.11.1]

BARCLAY, ADAM, MA, minister at Leochel and Cushnie Aberdeenshire, from 1606 until 1622. [F.VI.135]

BARCLAY, CHRISTIAN, spouse of John Forbes minister at Alford, Aberdeenshire, a sasine, 29 July 1601. [NRS.RS1.170]

BARCLAY, GEORGE, of Major Burnett's Troop of Dragoons, from Aberdeenshire, was mustered at Stirling on 10 December 1692. [FBL.295]

BARCLAY, ROBERT, of Syde, Strathcathro, Angus, testament, 1635, Comm. Brechin. [NRS]

BARNET, ANDREW, a militiaman in Kingoldrum, Angus, 1643. [NRS.GD16.50.17.4]

BARNET, DAVID, in Little Derry, Glen Isla, Angus, husband of Helen Elliot, testament, 1614, Comm. Brechin. [NRS]

BARNET, DAVID, , a militiaman in Kingoldrum, Angus, 1643. [NRS.GD16.50.17.4]

BARNET, JAMES, in Meikle Derry, Glen Isla, Angus, husband of Janet Cook, testament, 1614, Comm. Brechin. [NRS]

BARNET, JAMES, in Over Drumflogue, Glen Isla, Angus, testament, 1621, Comm. Brechin. [NRS]

BARNET, JOHN, a militiaman in Kingoldrum, Angus, 1643. [NRS.GD16.50.17.4]

BARNET, JOHN, in Westerton, a militiaman in Lintrathen, Angus, 1643. [NRS.GD16.50.17.4]

BARNET, JOHN, in Derry, Angus, testament, 1667, Comm. Brechin. [NRS]

BARNET, PATRICK, in Little Derry, Glen Isla, Angus, testament, 1613, Comm. Brechin. [NRS]

BARNET, THOMAS, a militiaman in Kingoldrum, Angus, 1643. [NRS.GD16.50.17.4]

BARNET, THOMAS, in Cant's Mill, husband of Elspet Cardean, born 1620, died 1644. [Airlie gravestone, Angus]

BARNSDAILLE, THOMAS, in Ege, Cortachy, Angus, testament, 1637, Comm. Brechin. [NRS]

BARRIE, DONALD, a tailor in Glen Muick, Aberdeenshire, in 1696. [PT]

BAXTER, ANDREW, born 1567, in Weltoun of Airlie, Angus, died on 25 May 1649, husband of Janet Mustard, born 1595, died 26 August 1656. [Airlie gravestone, Angus]

BAXTER, ANDREW, at the Kirk of Airlie, Angus, formerly in the Mains of Airlie, husband of Margaret Wilson, a sasine, 1672. [NRS.RS35. IV.206]

BARNETT, DAVID, in Lintrathen, Angus, 1691. [NRS.E69.11.1]

BARRONE, ALEXANDER, of Major Burnett's Troop of Dragoons, from Aberdeenshire, was mustered at Stirling on 10 December 1692. [FBL.295]

BAXTER, ANDREW, a militiaman in Airlie, Angus, 1643. [NRS.GD16.50.17.4]

BAXTER, JAMES, a militiaman in Airlie, Angus, 1643. [NRS.GD16.50.17.4]

BAXTER, JOHN, from Kincardineshire, a soldier guarding the Scottish Regalia then in Dunottar Castle from Cromwell's Army from 1651-1652. [DR]

BAXTER, JOHN, in Airlie, Angus, 1691. [NRS.E69.11.1]

BAXTER, JOHN, portioner of Kirkhillocks, Glen Isla, Angus, husband of Katherine Tulloch, testament, 1612, Comm. Brechin. [NRS]

BAXTER, JOHN, a militiaman in Lintrathen, Angus, 1643. [NRS.GD16.50.17.4]

BAXTER, WILLIAM, a militiaman in Airlie, Angus, 1643. [NRS.GD16.50.17.4]

BAXTER, WILLIAM, in Airlie, Angus, 1691. [NRS.E69.11.1]

BEAN, GEORGE, in Lethnott-Lochlee, Angus, 1691. [NRS.E69.11.1]

BEATON, GEORGE, of the Earl of Airlie's Militia, Angus, 1670. [NRS.GD16.53.39]

BEATON, JAMES, at the Mill of Careston, Angus, a sasine, and his wife Margaret Symmer, 1686. [NRS.RS33.VIII.55/220]

BEATTY, ADAM, a tenant, with his wife, in Nethertoun, Glenbuchat, Aberdeenshire. [1696 Poll Tax]

BEATTY, JOHN, son of William Beatty the elder, in Nethertoun, Glenbuchat, Aberdeenshire. [1696 Poll Tax]

BEATTY, WILLIAM, a tenant, with his wife, in Badenyon, Glenbuchat, Aberdeenshire. [1696 Poll Tax]

BEATTY, WILLIAM, the elder, a tenant, with his wife, in Nethertoun, Glenbuchat, Aberdeenshire. [1696 Poll Tax]

BEATTY, WILLIAM, the younger, a widower, a tenant, in Nethertoun, Glenbuchat, Aberdeenshire. [1696 Poll Tax]

BECKNIE, JOHN, in Alyth in 1691. [Hearth Tax Roll] [NRS.E69.19.1]

BEG, WILLIAM, in Freuchie, Glen Isla, Angus, husband of Katherine Findlay, testament, 1629, Comm. Brechin. [NRS]

BELL, ALEXANDER, and his wife Isobel Peter, in Adecat, Strathcathro, Angus, testament, 1614, Comm. Brechin. [NRS]

BELL, DAVID, in Navar, Angus, 1691. [NRS.E69.11.1]

BELL, ROBERT, and his wife Grissel Symmer, in Dubton, Angus, testament, 1629, Comm. Brechin. [NRS]

BELL, THOMAS, a militiaman in Airlie, Angus, 1643. [NRS.GD16.50.17.4]

BELLIE, DAVID, in Lethnott-Lochlee, Angus, 1691. [NRS.E69.11.1]

BELLIE, JAMES, in Navar, Angus, 1691. [NRS.E69.11.1]

BENNIE, MITCHELL, in Airlie, Angus, 1691. [NRS.E69.11.1]

BENNIE, PATRICK, born 1675, schoolmaster in Laurencekirk, Kincardineshire, died on 10 February 1695. [Laurencekirk gravestone]

BENVES, RICHARD, of Major Burnett's Troop of Dragoons, from Aberdeenshire, was mustered at Stirling on 10 December 1692. [FBL.295]

BETH, JOHN, of Major Burnett's Troop of Dragoons, from Aberdeenshire, was mustered at Stirling on 10 December 1692. [FBL.295]

BISHOP, JAMES, from Kincardineshire, a soldier guarding the Scottish Regalia then in Dunottar Castle from Cromwell's Army from 1651-1652. [DR]

BISHOP, JOHN, in Dubitoun, Fearn, Angus, a sasine, 1655. [NRS.RS34.IV.529]

BLACK, ANDREW, in Fearn, Angus, 1691. [NRS.E69.11.1]

BLACK, GEORGE, in Fearn, Angus, 1691. [NRS.E69.11.1]

BLACK, JAMES, in Lethnott-Lochlee, Angus, 1691. [NRS.E69.11.1]

BLACK, JOHN, from Kincardineshire, a soldier guarding the Scottish Regalia, then in Dunottar Castle besieged by Cromwell's Army from 1651 to 1652.

BLACK, JOHN, in Fearn, Angus, 1691. [NRS.E69.11.1]

BLAIKETER, JAMES, of Major Burnett's Troop of Dragoons, from Aberdeenshire, was mustered at Stirling on 10 December 1692. [FBL.295]

BLAIR, ALEXANDER, of Balthyock, a contract, 31 July 1607. [NRS.GD83.39]

BLAIR, BARBARA, in Alyth, Perthshire, in 1691. [Hearth Tax Roll] [NRS.E69.19.1]

BLAIR, GEORGE, the steward in Lord Ogilvie's house, Cortachy, Angus, militia list, 1643. [NRS.GD16.50.17.4]

BLAIR, JOHN, in Cortachy and Clova, Angus, 1691. [NRS.E69.11.1]

BLAIR, THOMAS, in Blairgowrie, Perthshire, in 1691. [Hearth Tax Roll] [NRS.E69.19.1]

BLAIR, WILLIAM, in Fearn, Angus, 1691. [NRS.E69.11.1]

BOIG, ANDREW, in Blairgowrie, Perthshire, in 1691. [Hearth Tax Roll] [NRS.E69.19.1]

BOIG, GEORGE, in Blairgowrie, Perthshire, in 1691. [Hearth Tax Roll] [NRS.E69.19.1]

BOIG, JOHN, in Blairgowrie, Perthshire, in 1691. [Hearth Tax Roll] [NRS.E69.19.1]

BONIBOY, WILLIAM, from Kincardineshire, a soldier guarding the Scottish Regalia then in Dunottar Castle from Cromwell's Army from 1651-1652. [DR]

BOTHE, WILLIAM, in Kirkburn of Cortachy, Angus, testament, 1633, Comm. Brechin. [NRS]

BOWER, ALEXANDER, of Kincaldrum, Angus, a deed, 1696. [NRS.RD2.80.i.412]

BOWMAN, JOHN, in Lethnott-Lochlee, Angus, 1691. [NRS.E69.11.1]

BOY, WILLIAM, a tenant in Glen Buchat, Aberdeenshire. [1696 Poll Tax]

BRABINER, or MCAVADINACH, JOHN, and his wife Isobel McNicoll, in Ballamanuch, Glen Isla, Angus, testament, 1696, Comm. Brechin. [NRS]

BRABNER, MARGARET, a sub-tenant in Ellenmore in the parish of Kindrochit/Braemar, Aberdeenshire, in 1696. [PT]

BRABNER, WILLIAM, a merchant in Fettercairn, Kincardineshire, a deed, 15 December 1618. [NRS.GD49.397]

BRAIKIE, MARGARET, servant of Harry Farquharson of Bellatrach, Glen Muick, Aberdeenshire, in 1696. [PT]

BRAND, ALEXANDER, born 1644, at the Mill of Glenbervie, died 16 July 1714. [Glenbervie gravestone, Kincardineshire]

BREBNER, JOHN, servant to Lady Jean Douglas or Gordon in Glenbuchat, Aberdeenshire. [1696 Poll Tax]

BRECHIN, ROBERT, servitor to Alexander Alexander, in Strathcathro, Angus, testament, 1637, Comm. Brechin. [NRS]

BRECK, JOHN, in Tilliequhillie, Navar, Angus, testament, 1627, Comm. Brechin. [NRS]

BROCK, ROBERT, in Tillearblit, Navar, Angus, husband of Katherine Chrystie, testament, 1611, Comm. Brechin. [NRS]

BRODIE, JOHN, from Kincardineshire, a soldier guarding the Scottish Regalia then in Dunottar Castle from Cromwell's Army from 1651-1652. [DR]

BROWN, ANDREW, a militiaman in Schanelie, Lintrathen, Angus, 1643. [NRS.GD16.50.17.4]

BROWN, ANDREW, from Strichen, Aberdeenshire, a sailor aboard the St Andrew, died at Darien, Panama, in 1698, testament 1707 Comm. Edinburgh. [NRS]

BROUN, GEORGE, in Tarland, Aberdeenshire, in 1696. [PT]

BROUN, ISABEL, in Little Dunkeld, Perthshire, in 1691. [Hearth Tax Records] [NRS.E69.19.1]

BROUN, JAMES, in Alyth, Perthshire, a deed, June 1624. [NRS.GD16.12.91]; renounced his claim to land in the barony of Alyth on 9 May 1624, to Lord James Ogilvy. [NRS.GD16.12.41]

BROUN, JAMES, in Edzell, Angus, 1691. [NRS.E69.11.1]

BROWN, JAMES, schoolmaster in Cortachy and Clova, Angus, 1691. [NRS.E69.11.1]

BROUN, JOHN, born 1602, in 'Kearlenwale', died on 15 June 1682. [Airlie gravestone, Angus]

BROUN, JOHN, in Airlie, Angus, 1691. [NRS.E69.11.1]

BROWN, ROBERT, of Major Burnett's Troop of Dragoons, from Aberdeenshire, was mustered at Stirling on 10 December 1692. [FBL.295]

BRUCE, JAMES, and his wife Janet Glen, in Rottuall, Angus, testament, 1613, Comm. Brechin. [NRS]

BRUCE, JAMES, in Forth, Glen Isla, Angus, testament, 1621, Comm. Brechin. [NRS]

BRUCE, JAMES, in Auchloch, Lochlee, Angus, husband of Bessie Chrystie, testament, 1627, Comm. Brechin. [NRS]

BRUCE, ALEXANDER, a cotter, and his wife Christian Alexander, in Over Bracow, Navar, Angus, testament, 1611, Comm. Brechin. [NRS]

BRUCE, ALEXANDER, of the Earl of Airlie's Militia, Angus, 1670. [NRS.GD16.53.39]

BRUCE, ANDREW, a militiaman in Fichill, Cortachy, Angus, 1643. [NRS.GD16.50.17.4]

BRUCE, ANDREW, versus the Earl of Aboyne, Aberdeenshire, in 1683. [NRS.CS230.B.1.13]

BRUCE, JAMES, born 1666, tenant in Westside, died 1738, father of David, James, Isobel, John, Agnes, Margaret, Katherine, Jean, Robert, and Mary. [Edzell gravestone, Angus]

BRUCE, JAMES, in Alyth, Perthshire, in 1691. [Hearth Tax Roll] [NRS.E69.19.1]

BRUCE, JOHN, in Alrick, Glen Isla, Angus, husband of Christian Pressan, testament, 1626, Comm. Brechin. [NRS]

BRUCE, THOMAS, in Ledincarre, Fearn, Angus, testament, 1601, Comm. Brechin. [NRS]

BRUCE, THOMAS, in Cureford, Navar, Angus, husband of Katherine Anderson, testament, 1611, Comm. Brechin. [NRS]

BRUNACH, JOHN, a servant of Robert Milne in Milltown of Glen Buchat, Aberdeenshire. [1696 Poll Tax]

BUCHAN, JOHN, in Edzell, Angus, 1691. [NRS.E69.11.1]

BUMAN, JOHN, a tenant in Tombae, Glen Muick, Aberdeenshire, in 1696. [PT]

BURGESS, JOHN, of Major Burnett's Troop of Dragoons, from Aberdeenshire, was mustered at Stirling on 10 December 1692. [FBL.295]

BURN, ALEXANDER, in Fearn, Angus, 1691. [NRS.E69.11.1]

BURN, WILLIAM, in Auchenlish, Glen Isla, Angus, his widow Elspet McNicoll, testament, 1662, Comm. Brechin. [NRS]

BURNES, JAMES, born 1656, tenant of Bralinmuir, died on 23 January 1743, husband of Margaret Falconer, born 1659, died 28 December 1749. [Glenbervie gravestone, Kincardineshire]

BURNETT, AGNES, spouse of Alexander Spalding in Lochend, heir of John Burnett, a burgess of Brechin, Angus, 26 July 1661. [BrMS2/1/1/9]

BURNETT, ALEXANDER, of Leys, Aberdeenshire, was granted the lands of Pittenkeirie and the tithes of the parish church of Banchory Ternan by James, Marquis of Hamilton on 13 May 1614. [FBL.219]

BURNETT, CHRISTIAN, spouse of John Balfour, gardener in Fetteresso, heir of John Burnett, a burgess of Brechin, Angus, 26 July 1661. [BrMS2/1/1/9]

BURNETT, DAVID, in Lintrathen, Angus, 1691. [NRS.E69.11.1]

BURNETT, JANET, wife of Sir Alexander Cumming of Coulter, testament confirmed on 2 October 1669. [NRS.Comm. Aberdeen]

BURNETT, ROBERT, MA, minister of Banchory Ternan, Kincardineshire, from 1682 until 1695. [F.6.80]

BURNETT, ROBERT, of Glenbervie, Kincardineshire, a deed in 1696. [NRS.79.23]

BURNETT, Sir THOMAS, of Leys, purchased the lands of Livingstoun Donypace near Argul Bay, in Nova Scotia from Sir William Alexander of Menstrie on 7 November 1625. On 21 April 1626 King Charles I created Sir Thomas as the Knight Baronet of the lands, Barony and Regality of Leisburnet in Nova Scotia [FBL.227-231; 232-256]; he subscribed his will at Leyis on 8 December 1652. [FBL.277-284]

BURNETT, Captain WILLIAM, a muster roll of his company [of Militia?] at Fettercairn, Kincardineshire, in 1692. [NRS.E10024.5]; at Stirling in 1692. [FBL.295]

BURNETT, ..., of Leys, versus Irvine of Drum, a decreet of exoneration, dated 1692. [NRS.CS142.15]

BURRY, JOHN, in Inver Kinnaird, born about 1680, died on 25 April 1740. [Little Dunkeld gravestone, Perthshire]

BUTTER, ANDREW, a militiaman in Lintrathen, Angus, 1643. [NRS.GD16.50.17.4]

BUTTER, ANDREW, in Goventar, Glen Isla, Angus, husband of Margaret Ramsay, testament, 1654, Comm. Brechin. [NRS]

BUTTER, JOHN, a militiaman in Lintrathen, Angus, 1643. [NRS.GD16.50.17.4]

BUTTER, JOHN, in Blairgowrie, Perthshire, in 1691. [Hearth Tax Roll] [NRS.E69.19.1]

BUTTER, THOMAS, in Blairgowrie, Perthshire, in 1691. [Hearth Tax Roll] [NRS.E69.19.1]

CAB, JOHN, in Navar, Angus, 1691. [NRS.E69.11.1]

CADDELL, ALEXANDER, a tenant in Graystone, Glen Muick, Aberdeenshire, in 1696. [PT]

CADDELL, ANNA, a sub-tenant in the parish of Crathie, Aberdeenshire, in 1696. [PT]

CADDELL, JOHN, in Arntibber, Clova, Angus, militia list, 1643. [NRS.GD16.50.17.4]

CADDELL, JOHN, from Kincardineshire, a soldier guarding the Scottish Regalia then in Dunottar Castle from Cromwell's Army from 1651-1652. [DR]

CAIRD, DAVID, in Pitreichie, husband of Jean Grige born 1663, died 10 November 1730. [Glenbervie gravestone, Kincardineshire]

CAIRD, JOHN, born 1656, in Kaebogg, died 17 September 1722, husband of Jean Millen, born 1658, died 18 November 1743. [Glenbervie gravestone, Kincardineshire]

CALDER, ALEXANDER, in Coullie, in the parish of Coull, Aberdeenshire, 1696. [PT]

CALDER, ELSPET, in Easter Cults, in Tarland, Aberdeenshire, in 1696. [PT]

CALDER, WILLIAM, in Easter Cults, in Tarland, Aberdeenshire, in 1696. [PT]

CALLAN, ALASTER, with his wife, in Uppertoun, Glen Buchat, Aberdeenshire. [1696 Poll Tax]

CAMPBELL, ALEXANDER, of Major Burnett's Troop of Dragoons, from Aberdeenshire, was mustered at Stirling on 10 December 1692. [FBL.295]

CAMPBELL, COLIN, portioner of Innerarity, Glen Isla, Angus, and his wife Elspet Suttie, testament, 1634, Comm. Brechin. [NRS]

CAMPBELL, DAVID, born 1619, son of Reverend Colin Campbell in Dundee, graduated MA from St Andrews in 1639, minister of Menmuir, Angus, from 1644 to his death in 1696, husband of Magdalen Livingston, parents of Colin and James. [F.5.408]; testament, 1705, Comm. Brechin. [NRS]

CAMPBELL, JAMES, of the Earl of Airlie's Militia, Angus, 1670. [NRS.GD16.53.39]

CAMPBELL, JOHN, in Airlie, Angus, 1691. [NRS.E69.11.1]

CANDOW, WILLIAM, a fencibleman in Holl, Lintrathen, Angus, 1643. [NRS.GD16.50.17.4]

CANT, ALEXANDER, son of Andrew Cant in Aberdeen, graduated MA from King's College in Aberdeen in 1636, minister at Banchory Ternan, Kincardineshire, from 1646 until deposed in 1651, he died on 30 March 1665. [F.6.80]

CARDEAN, DAVID, born 1588, died 3 May 1662, husband of Elspet Stil, born 1594, died on 4 June 1662. [Airlie gravestone, Angus]

CARDEAN, ELSPET, born 1620, wife of Thomas Barnet in Cantsmill, died on 8 April 1644. [Airlie gravestone, Angus]

CARGILL, DONALD, in Blairgowrie, Perthshire, in 1691. [Hearth Tax Roll] [NRS.E69.19.1]

CARGILL, JOHN, in Meikle Derry, Glen Isla, Angus, testament, 1662, Comm. Brechin. [NRS]

CARMAIG, ALEXANDER, in Drumflogne, Glen Isla, Angus, husband of Isobel Storrer, testament, 1610, Comm. Brechin. [NRS]

CARMOCK, JOHN, in Broklhoss, Cortachy, Angus, husband of Christian Millar, testament, 1637, Comm. Brechin. [NRS]

CARNEGIE, Sir ALEXANDER, of Balnamoon, Angus, husband of Giles Blair, a sasine, 1648. [NRS.RS34.III.12]

CARNEGIE, JAMES, of Balnamoon, Angus, a bond, 23 February 1672. [NRS.GD16.1.81.4]

CARNEGIE, JAMES, of Braikie, and Anna Ogilvy, eldest daughter of Sir David Ogilvy of Innerquharity, Angus, a marriage contract, 1686. [NRS.GD205.box 12, bundle 33]

CARNEGIE, ANDREW, born 1641, in Moortoun, died 1714. [Fearn gravestone, Angus]

CARNEGIE, JAMES, of Finavon, Angus, deeds in 1696. [NRS.RD4.78.478/1144]

CARNEGIE, JOHN, born 1655, in Inchbrake, did 20 December 1735, husband of Margaret Kinneir, born 1670, died 12 February 1730. [Glenbervie gravestone, Kincardineshire]

CARNOCT, JOHN, a militiaman in Lintrathen, Angus, 1643. [NRS.GD16.50.17.4]

CARNOCT, JOHN, the younger, a militiaman in Lintrathen, Angus, 1643. [NRS.GD16.50.17.4]

CARVER, JAMES, in Blairgowrie, Perthshire, in 1691. [Hearth Tax Roll] [NRS.E69.19.1]

CATANACH, ALASTER, a sub-tenant in the parish of Crathie, Aberdeenshire, in 1696. [PT]

CAY, JOHN, in Lintrathen, Angus, 1691. [NRS.E69.11.1]

CHALMERS, GEORGE, in Blairgowrie, Perthshire, in 1691. [Hearth Tax Roll] [NRS.E69.19.1]

CHALMERS, JOHN, in Alyth, Perthshire, in 1691. [Hearth Tax Roll] [NRS.E69.19.1]

CHALMERS, WILLIAM, in Blairgowrie, Perthshire, in 1691. [Hearth Tax Roll] [NRS.E69.19.1]

CHAPLAND, ANDREW, in Edzell, Angus, 1691. [NRS.E69.11.1]

CHAPLAIN, JOHN, husband of Elaine Small, in Kingoldrum, Angus, parents of John Chaplain, born 1637, died 1659. [Airlie gravestone, Angus]

CHAPLAIN, WILLIAM, in Menmuir, Angus, 1691. [NRS.E69.11.1]

CHRISTIE, ALEXANDER, in Lethnott-Lochlee, Angus, 1691. [NRS.E69.11.1]

CHRISTIE, CHARLES, in Edzell, Angus, 1691. [NRS.E69.11.1]

CHRISTIE, DAVID, in Edzell, Angus, 1691. [NRS.E69.11.1]

CHRISTIE, DAVID, in Lethnott-Lochlee, Angus, 1691. [NRS.E69.11.1]

CHRISTIE, JAMES, in Edzell, Angus, 1691. [NRS.E69.11.1]

CHRISTIE, JOHN, a militiaman at Brigend, Lintrathen, Angus, 1643. [NRS.GD16.50.17.4]

CHRISTIE, JOHN, son of Alexander Christie in Alford, Aberdeenshire, was apprenticed to Patrick Christie the eder, a burgess of Aberdeen in 1664. [ACA]

CHRISTIE, JOHN, in Edzell, Angus, 1691. [NRS.E69.11.1]

CHRYSTIE, JOHN, in Lintrathen, Angus, 1691. [NRS.E69.11.1]

CHRISTIE, WILLIAM, and his wife Katherine Christison, in Whiggintoun, Lochlee, Angus, testament, 1636, Comm. Brechin. [NRS]

CHRISTIE, WILLIAM, aged 70, husband of Margaret Davidson, aged 70, died 16… [Fettercairn gravestone, Kincardineshire]

CHRISTISON, ALEXANDER, in Lethnott-Lochlee, Angus, 1691. [NRS.E69.11.1]

CHRISTISON, JOHN, in Assailzie, Lochlee, Angus, testament, 1627, Comm. Brechin. [NRS]

CHRISTISON, JOHN, and his wife Janet Christison, in Milton of Glenesk, Angus, testament, 1627, Comm. Brechin. [NRS]

CHRISTISON, JOHN, son of the late John Christison, in Milton of Lochlee, Angus, testament, 1627, Comm. Brechin. [NRS]

CHRISTISON, JAMES, in Edzell, Angus, 1691. [NRS.E69.11.1]

CHRISTISON, JOHN, in Lethnott-Lochlee, Angus, 1691. [NRS.E69.11.1]

CHRISTISON, THOMAS, in Edzell, Angus, 1691. [NRS.E69.11.1]

CLEPHAN, ANDREW, in Edzell, Angus, 1691. [NRS.E69.11.1]

CLERK, ALEXANDER, a cottar and a militiaman in Inchin, Lintrathen, Angus, 1643. [NRS.GD16.50.17.4]

CLERK, A., of the Earl of Airlie's Militia, Angus, 1670. [NRS.GD16.53.39]

CLARK, DAVID, in Newton of Glen Isla, Angus, testament, 1662, Comm. Brechin. [NRS]

CLERK, DAVID, in Lintrathen, Angus, 1691. [NRS.E69.11.1]

CLERK, GEORGE, in Westerton, a militiaman in Lintrathen, Angus, 1643. [NRS.GD16.50.17.4]

CLARK, JAMES, in Holmuir, Glen Isla, Angus, husband of Margaret Paterson, testament, 1625, Comm. Brechin. [NRS]

CLERK, JAMES, from Kincardineshire, a soldier guarding the Scottish Regalia then in Dunottar Castle from Cromwell's Army from 1651-1652. [DR]

CLERK, JOHN, a militiaman in Schanelie, Lintrathen, Angus, 1643. [NRS.GD16.50.17.4]

CLERK, JOHN, in Lethnott-Lochlee, Angus, 1691. [NRS.E69.11.1]

CLERK, JOHN, in Alyth, Perthshire, in 1691. [Hearth Tax Roll] [NRS.E69.19.1]

CLERK, JOHN, in Middle Todd, a militiaman in Lintrathen, Angus, 1643. [NRS.GD16.50.17.4]

CLARK, JOHN, in Frecaye, Glen Isla, Angus, husband of Agnes Ford, testament, 1662, Comm. Brechin. [NRS]

CLARK, MARGARET, in Clova, Angus, testament, 1667, Comm. Brechin. [NRS]

CLERK, PATRICK, in Cortachy and Clova, Angus, 1691. [NRS.E69.11.1]

CLERK, RICHARD, in Glenmarkie, barony of Glen Isla, Angus, 1667. [RGS.XI.1105]

CLERK, RICHARD, in Nether Auchinleiss, Glen Isla, Angus, husband of Margaret Breischane, testament, 1695, Comm. Brechin. [NRS]

CLERK, RICHARD, in the barony of Glenisla, Perthshire, in 1663. [RGS.XI.464]

CLARK, RICHARD, from Kincardineshire, a soldier guarding the Scottish Regalia then in Dunottar Castle from Cromwell's Army from 1651-1652. [DR]

CLARK, ROBERT, in Frewch, Glen Isla, Perthshire, husband of Bessie Herreall, testament, 1625, Comm. Brechin. [NRS]

CLERK, THOMAS, a militiaman in Pitmidie, Lintrathen, Angus, 1643. [NRS.GD16.50.17.4]

CLERK, THOMAS, in Glenisla, Angus, 1691. [NRS.E69.11.1]

CLERK, WILLIAM, in Westerton, a militiaman in Lintrathen, Angus, 1643. [NRS.GD16.50.17.4]

CLERK, WILLIAM, in Lintrathen, Angus, 1691. [NRS.E69.11.1]

CLERK, WILLIAM, of Major Burnett's Troop of Dragoons, from Aberdeenshire, was mustered at Stirling on 3 December 1697. [FBL.295]

COBB, JOHN, in Tilliarblet, Navar, Angus, wife Janet Milne, testament, 1685, Comm. Brechin. [NRS]

COLLACE, JOHN, heir to his grandfather John Collace of Balnamoon, Angus, in lands in the barony of Menmuir, 1632. [NRS.Retours]

COLLIE, JAMES, from Kincardineshire, a soldier guarding the Scottish Regalia then in Dunottar Castle from Cromwell's Army from 1651-1652. [DR]

COLLIE, JOHN, in Over Alrick, Glen Isla, Angus, a testament, 1621, Comm. Brechin. [NRS]

CONDACH, JAMES, a tenant, with his wife, in Backhillock, Glen Buchat, Aberdeenshire, in 1696. [PT]

CONDACH, JOHN, a tenant, in Backhillock, Glen Buchat, Aberdeenshire, in1696. [PT]

CONSTABLE, or GLENDY, AGNES, born 1674, died 1732, mother of Andrew Glendy. [Airlie gravestone, Angus]

COOK, ALEXANDER, in Blairgowrie, Perthshire, in 1691. [Hearth Tax Roll] [NRS.E69.19.1]

COOK, EDWARD, in Dykehead of Craig, Glen Isla, Angus, testament, 1637, Comm. Brechin. [NRS]

COOK, JAMES, a militiaman in Schanellie, Lintrathen, Angus, 1643. [NRS.GD16.50.17.4]

COPLAND, PATRICK, was educated at Marischal College in Aberdeen, minister at Cushnie, Aberdeenshire, from 1672 until his death in 1710, husband of Jean Gordon. [F.VI.137]

COPLAND, JANET, in Menmuir, Angus, 1691.
[NRS.E69.11.1]

CORBE, JOHN, in Cortachy and Clova, Angus, 1691.
[NRS.E69.11.1]

CORRIONRE, JAMES, a militiaman in Airlie, Angus, 1643.
[NRS.GD16.50.17.4]

COSSINS, JOHN, in Lintrathen, Angus, 1691. [NRS.E69.11.1]

COSSON, JOHN, in Cortachy and Clova, Angus, 1691.
[NRS.E69.11.1]

COUPAR, DAVID, in Lord Ogilvie's house, Cortachy, Angus, militia list, 1643. [NRS.GD16.50.17.4]

COUPAR, ELSPET, a widow, in Badenyon, Glenbuchat, Aberdeenshire. [1696 Poll Tax]

COUTTS, ROBERT, of Auchtercoull, sold the lands of Auchtercoull to Sir Alexander Irvine of Drum in 1633, a Royal Charter. [NRS.GD33.11/13]

COUTS, THOMAS, in Mill of Kincraig in Tarland, Aberdeenshire, in 1696. [PT]

COUTTS, WILLIAM, in Clova, Angus, militia list, 1643.
[NRS.GD16.50.17.4]

COUTS, WILLIAM, a servant in the parish of Crathie, Aberdeenshire, in 1696. [PT]

COWIE, ALEXANDER, born 1630, of the Mill of Halkerton, died in March 1709, husband of Margaret Beattie. [Laurencekirk gravestone, Kincardineshire]

COWIE, ROBERT, in Lethnot, Angus, testament, 1628, Comm. Brechin. [NRS]

CRAIG, GEORGE, a militiaman in Braeside, Cortachy, Angus, 1643. [NRS.GD16.50.17.4]

CRAICK, JOHN, born 1669, farmer at Brea of Old Allan, died 1740, husband of Margaret Davidson, parents of James. [Lintrathen gravestone, Angus]

CRAIG, GILBERT, from Kincardineshire, a soldier guarding the Scottish Regalia then in Dunottar Castle from Cromwell's Army from 1651 to 1652. [DR]

CRAIG, WILLIAM, in Alyth, Perthshire, in 1691. [Hearth Tax Roll] [NRS.E69.19.1]

CRAIK, THOMAS, in Clova, Angus, militia list, 1643. [NRS.GD16.50.17.4]

CRAMOND, JAMES, graduated MA from King's College, Aberdeen, in 1644, minister of Fearn, Angus, from 1653 until his death in 1690, husband of Geils Ramsay, parents of William, James, and Elizabeth. [F.5.396]

CRAWFORD, JOHN, from Kincardineshire, a soldier guarding the Scottish Regalia then in Dunottar Castle from Cromwell's Army from 1651-1652. [DR]

CRICHTON, ANDREW, a militiaman in Pitmidie, Lintrathen, Angus, 1643. [NRS.GD16.50.17.4]

CRICHTON, DAVID, in Caldhame, Clova, Angus, husband of Margaret Shirrell, testament, 1700, Comm. Brechin. [NRS]

CRICHTON, JAMES, and his wife Isobel Ogilvy, in Easter Overcraig, Glen Isla, Angus, testament, 1667, Comm. Brechin. [NRS]

CRICHTON, JOHN, in Drumflogue, Glen Isla, Angus, testament, 1621, Comm. Brechin. [NRS]

CRIGHTON, ANDREW, in Airlie, Angus, 1691. [NRS.E69.11.1]

CRIGHTON, DAVID, in Cookston, Airlie, Angus, 1691. [NRS.E69.11.1]

CRIGHTON, JAMES, in Linross in Airlie, Angus, 1691. [NRS.E69.11.1]

CRIGHTON, JOHN, in Blairgowrie, Perthshire, in 1691. [Hearth Tax Roll] [NRS.E69.19.1]

CRIGHTON, PATRICK, sr. and jr., in Airlie, Angus, 1691. [NRS.E69.11.1]

CROKAT, DONALD, in Lord Ogilvie's house, Cortachy, Angus, militia list, 1643. [NRS.GD16.50.17.4]

CROCKETT, HENDRIE, in Edzell, Angus, 1691. [NRS.E69.11.1]

CROCKETT, HENRY, in Lethnott-Lochlee, Angus, 1691. [NRS.E69.11.1]

CROCKETT, JAMES, in Lintrathen, Angus, 1691. [NRS.E69.11.1]

CROFTS, DAVID, in Fearn, Angus, 1691. [NRS.E69.11.1]

CROLL, ALEXANDER, in Edzell, Angus, 1691. [NRS.E69.11.1]

CROMAR, JOHN, in Wardfald, in the parish of Coull, Aberdeenshire, 1696. [PT]

CRUICKSHANK, ALEXANDER, of Major Burnett's Troop of Dragoons, from Aberdeenshire, was mustered at Stirling on 10 December 1692. [FBL.295]

CRUICKSHANK, JOHN, born 14 April 1693, son of Robert Cruickshank in Ruthven, Strathbogie, was baptised there by Father Robert Francis on 15 April 1693. [SNQ.VIII.181]

CRUICKSHANK, WILLIAM, schoolmaster in Aboyne, Aberdeenshire, 1682. [NRS.RD2.57.799]

CUPAR, ANDREW, in Fearn, Angus, 1691. [NRS.E69.11.1]

CUSHNIE, ANDREW, a servant of the Laird of Drum in Aberdeenshire, was baptised a Catholic by Father Robert Francis on 29 March 1698. [SNQ.VIII.182]

DAIRE, JOHN, from Kincardineshire, a soldier guarding the Scottish Regalia then in Dunottar Castle from Cromwell's Army from 1651-1652. [DR]

DALGETTY, JOHN, in Lethnott-Lochlee, Angus, 1691. [NRS.E69.11.1]

DALGETTY, DAVID, in Drumcairn, Lethnot, Angus, husband of Katherine Gold, testament, 1631, Comm. Brechin. [NRS]

DANYE, ELSPET, died in 1605, wife of George Fasyid. [Kearn gravestone, Aberdeenshire]

DAVID, JOHN, in Little Dunkeld, Perthshire, in 1691. [Hearth Tax Records] [NRS.E69.19.1]

DAVIDSON, ALEXANDER, and his wife Margaret Nicoll, in Drumcairn, Lethnot, Angus, testament, 1693, Comm. Brechin. [NRS]

DAVIDSON, ISOBEL, in Alyth, Perthshire, in 1691. [Hearth Tax Roll] [NRS.E69.19.1]

DAVIDSON, JOHN, a militiaman at Campsie, Lintrathen, Angus, 1643. [NRS.GD16.50.17.4]

DAVIDSON, NORMAND, of Balnacraig, Aboyne, Aberdeenshire, 1667. [AVR]

DAVIDSON, Sir WILLIAM, was granted the lands of Fettercairn, Kincardineshire, on 3 February 1671. [NRS.SIG.38.141]

DAVIE, JAMES, in Cortachy and Clova, Angus, 1691. [NRS.E69.11.1]

DAVISON, JOHN, of Major Burnett's Troop of Dragoons, from Aberdeenshire, was mustered at Stirling on 3 December 1697. [FBL.295]

DENS, JOHN, husband of Isabel Macher, born 1675, died 1713. [Lintrathen gravestone, Angus]

DESON, ALASTER, a cottar, with his wife, in Glenbuchat, Aberdeenshire. [1696 Poll Tax]

DESON, JAMES, a tenant, with his wife in Backhillock, Glen Buchat, Aberdeenshire. [1696 Poll Tax]

DEUCHARS, ALEXANDER, in Fearn, Angus, 1691. [NRS.E69.11.1]

DEUCHARS, DAVID, in Fearn, Angus, 1691. [NRS.E69.11.1]

DEUCHARS, JAMES, in Fearn, Angus, 1691. [NRS.E69.11.1]

DEVNEY, PATRICK, a miller in Balmoral, in the parish of Crathie, Aberdeenshire, in 1696. [PT]

DICK, Sergeant JOHN, of Major Burnett's Troop of Dragoons was mustered at Stirling on 16 Decembe 1692, was discharged in Inverness on 3 December 1697. [FBL.295]

DICKIE, A., from Kincardineshire, a soldier guarding the Scottish Regalia then in Dunottar Castle from Cromwell's Army from 1651-1652. [DR]

DICKIE, JOHN, from Kincardineshire, a soldier guarding the Scottish Regalia then in Dunottar Castle from Cromwell's Army from 1651-1652. [DR]

DICKSON, JOHN, born 1611, in Little Kenny, died 1695, husband of Janet Wright. [Lintrathen gravestone, Angus]

DICKSON, WILLIAM, a Notary Public in Cortachy and Clova, Angus, 1691. [NRS.E69.11.1]

DINGWALL, GEORGE, versus Irvine of Drum, Aberdeenshire, on 20 July 1699. [NRS.CS96.26]

DOIG, JOHN, in Lintrathen, Angus, 1691. [NRS.E69.11.1]

DOIG, WILLIAM, a militiaman in Kinloch, Lintrathen, Angus, 1643. [NRS.GD16.50.17.4]

DOIG, WILLIAM, in Airlie, Angus, 1691. [NRS.E69.11.1]

DON, ALEXANDER, at the Kirk of Menmuir, Angus, testament, 1652, Comm. Brechin. [NRS]

DON, ALEXANDER, in Alyth, Perthshire, in 1691. [Hearth Tax Roll] [NRS.E69.19.1]

DON, JOHN, in Meikle Derry, Glen Isla, Angus, husband of Christian Mastertoun, testaments, 1624, 1628, Comm. Brechin. [NRS]

DON, JOHN, son of the late John Don, in Meikle Derry, Glen Isla, Angus, testament, 1642, Comm. Brechin. [NRS]

DON, JOHN, in Edzell, Angus, 1691. [NRS.E69.11.1]

DON, THOMAS, of Dalbog, died 1672, husband of Agnes Stewart, died 1686, parents of Elizabeth, died 1661. [Edzell gravestone, Angus]

DONALD, ALEXANDER, and his wife Margaret Mitchell, in Fedderage, testament, 1611, Comm. Brechin. [NRS]

DONALD, ALEXANDER, and his wife Annas Edward in Glen Moy, Angus, testament, 1628, Comm. Brechin. [NRS]

DONALD, ALEXANDER, a militiaman in Adelun, Cortachy, Angus, 1643. [NRS.GD16.50.17.4]

DONALD, ALEXANDER, and his wife Janet Froster, in Shank of Glen Moy, Angus, testament, 1657, Comm. Brechin. [NRS]

DONALD, DAVID, the younger, in Middle Todd, a militiaman in Lintrathen, Angus, 1643. [NRS.GD16.50.17.4]

DONALD, JAMES, and his wife Janet Fenton, in Ogie, Cortachy, testament, 1611, Comm. Brechin. [NRS]

DONALD, JOHN, a militiaman in Rottuell, Cortachy, Angus, 1643. [NRS.GD16.50.17.4]

DONALD, THOMAS, in Lintrathen, Angus, 1691. [NRS.E69.11.1]

DONALDSON, JAMES, in Edzell, Angus, 1691. [NRS.E69.11.1]

DONALDSON, JOHN, a militiaman at Brigend, Lintrathen, Angus, 1643. [NRS.GD16.50.17.4]

DONALDSON, JOHN, from Kincardineshire, a soldier guarding the Scottish Regalia then in Dúnottar Castle from Cromwell's Army from 1651-1652. [DR]

DONALDSON, JOHN, in Edzell, Angus, 1691. [NRS.E69.11.1]

DONALDSON, JOHN, in Lethnott-Lochlee, Angus, 1691. [NRS.E69.11.1]

DONALDSON, THOMAS, in Arntibber, Clova, Angus, militia list, 1643. [NRS.GD16.50.17.4]

DONETT, DAVID, in Cortachy and Clova, Angus, 1691. [NRS.E69.11.1]

DONETT, JAMES, in Cortachy and Clova, Angus, 1691. [NRS.E69.11.1]

DONETT, JOHN, in Lintrathen, Angus, 1691. [NRS.E69.11.1]

DONETT, JOHN, in Cortachy and Clova, Angus, 1691. [NRS.E69.11.1]

DOUBIE, JOHN, in Fearn, Angus, 1691. [NRS.E69.11.1]

DOUGLAS, DAVID, a militiaman at Purgavie, Lintrathan, Angus, 1643. [NRS.GD16.50.17.4]

DOUGLAS, JOHN, from Kincardineshire, a soldier guarding the Scottish Regalia then in Dunottar Castle from Cromwell's Army from 1651-1652. [DR]

DOUGLAS, MARGARET, spouse of William Forbes of Monymusk, Aberdeenshire, a sasine, 1603. [NRS.RS6.1.133]

DOUGLAS, WILLIAM, of Blackmiln, son of Thomas Douglas, a merchant in Aberdeen and his wife Bridget Forbes, was educated at Marischal College in Aberdeen from 1621 until 1625, minister at Aboyne and Glentanar, Aberdeenshire, from 1633 until 1648. [F.6.77]

DOUGLAS, Sir WILLIAM, of Glenbervie, Kincardineshire, a sasine, 27 August 1625, Nova Scotia. [NRS.RS1.18.124]

DOUGLAS, WILLIAM, an advocate, was granted the baronies of Airlie and of Cortachy, Angus, in 1666. [RGS.XI.968]

DOURIE, WILLIAM, in Navar, Angus, 1691. [NRS.E69.11.1]

DOW, JOHN, in Little Dunkeld, Perthshire, in 1691. [Hearth Tax Records] [NRS.E69.19.1]

DRUMMOND, JOHN, from Kincardineshire, a soldier guarding the Scottish Regalia then in Dunottar Castle from Cromwell's Army from 1651-1652. [DR]

DUNBAR, ALEXANDER, born 1686, of the Miltoun of Newmill, died 1729. [Kildrummy gravestone, Aberdeenshire]

DUNBAR, WILLIAM, a tenant, with his wife, in Badenyon, in Glenbuchat, Aberdeenshire, in1696. [PT]

DUNCAN, ALEXANDER, in Acharn, Clova, Angus, militia list, 1643. [NRS.GD16.50.17.4]

DUNCAN, ALEXANDER, a militiaman in Balloh, Cortachy, Angus, 1643. [NRS.GD16.50.17.4]

DUNCAN, ALEXANDER, son of Thomas Duncan in Kincardine O'Neill, Kincardineshire, was apprenticed to John Edward, a weaver in Aberdeen, in 1650. [ACA]

DUNCAN, ALEXANDER, in Cortachy and Clova, Angus, 1691. [NRS.E69.11.1]

DUNCAN, ALEXANDER, in Navar, Angus, 1691. [NRS.E69.11.1]

DUNCAN, DAVID, in Fearn, Angus, 1691. [NRS.E69.11.1]

DUNCAN, ISABEL, in Edzell, Angus, 1691. [NRS.E69.11.1]

DUNCAN, JAMES, in Bush, Clova, Angus, militia list, 1643. [NRS.GD16.50.17.4]

DUNCAN, JAMES, a militiaman in Balloh, Cortachy, Angus, 1643. [NRS.GD16.50.17.4]

DUNCAN, JOHN, a militiaman in Cordache, Lintrathen, Angus, 1643. [NRS.GD16.50.17.4]

DUNCAN, JOHN, the younger, in Clova, Angus, militia list, 1643. [NRS.GD16.50.17.4]

DUNCAN, JOHN, in Cortachy and Clova, Angus, 1691. [NRS.E69.11.1]

DUNCAN, JOHN, a shoemaker in Glen Muick, Aberdeenshire, in 1696. [PT]

DUNCAN, PATRICK, of Major Burnett's Troop of Dragoons, from Aberdeenshire, was mustered at Stirling on 3 December 1697. [FBL.295]

DUNCAN, ROBERT, a militiaman in Craigend, Cortachy, Angus, 1643. [NRS.GD16.50.17.4]

DUNCAN, THOMAS, and his wife Janet Young, in Flobeitt, Navar, Angus, testament, 1610, Comm. Brechin. [NRS]

DUNCAN, THOMAS, in Rottual, Cortachy, Angus, husband of Margaret Lindsay, testament, 1611, Comm. Brechin. [NRS]

DUNCAN, THOMAS, a militiaman in Lintrathen, Angus, 1643. [NRS.GD16.50.17.4]

DUNCAN, THOMAS, in Bracow, Navar, Angus, husband of Elspet Smart, testament, 1663, Comm. Brechin. [NRS]

DUNCAN, THOMAS, and his wife Barbara Smith, in Bracow, Navar, Angus, testament, 1674, Comm. Brechin. [NRS]

DUNCAN, THOMAS, in Cortachy and Clova, Angus, 1691. [NRS.E69.11.1]

DURIE, ALEXANDER, in Edzell, Angus, 1691. [NRS.E69.11.1]

DURIE, DAVID, in Lethnott-Lochlee, Angus, 1691. [NRS.E69.11.1]

DURWARD, ROBERT, in Tarland, Aberdeenshire, in 1696. [PT]

DURWARD, MALCOLM, in Teanlay in the parish of Coull, Aberdeenshire, 1696. [PT]

DYKERS, DAVID, in Menmuir, Angus, 1691. [NRS.E69.11.1]

EDISON, JOHN, in Kirkton of Clova, Angus, militia list, 1643. [NRS.GD16.50.17.4]

EDWARD, THOMAS, and his wife Agnes Knight, in Fichhill, Cortachy, Angus, testament, 1611, Comm. Brechin. [NRS]

EDWARD, ALEXANDER, in Cortachy and Clova, Angus, 1691. [NRS.E69.11.1]

EDWARD, ELSPET, a widow in Glen Prosen, Angus, testament, 16 October 1673, Comm. St Andrews. [NRS]

EDWARD, GEORGE, from Kincardineshire, a soldier guarding the Scottish Regalia then in Dunottar Castle from Cromwell's Army from 1651-1652. [DR]

EDWARD, JAMES, son of Thomas Edward, a militiaman in Raverny, Lintrathen, Angus, 1643. [NRS.GD16.50.17.4]

EDWARD, JOHN, a militiaman in Corssmell, Cortachy, Angus, 1643. [NRS.GD16.50.17.4]

EDWARD, JOHN, from Kincardineshire, a soldier guarding the Scottish Regalia then in Dunottar Castle from Cromwell's Army from 1651-1652. [DR]

EDWARD, JOHN, in Lethnott-Lochlee, Angus, 1691. [NRS.E69.11.1]

EDWARD, JOHN, in Lintrathen, Angus, 1691. [NRS.E69.11.1]

EDWARD, JOHN, in Cortachy and Clova, Angus, 1691. [NRS.E69.11.1]

EDWARD, ROBERT, in Lethnott-Lochlee, Angus, 1691. [NRS.E69.11.1]

EDWARD, THOMAS, in Bahood, Clova, Angus, militia list, 1643. [NRS.GD16.50.17.4]

EDWARD, THOMAS, a militiaman in Raverny, Lintrathen, Angus, 1643. [NRS.GD16.50.17.4]

EGO, WILLIAM, a tenant in the parish of Crathie, Aberdeenshire, in 1696. [PT]

ELDER, ROBERT, in Lethnott-Lochlee, Angus, 1691. [NRS.E69.11.1]

ELLAT, CHRISTIAN, relict of John Sanderis in Welton, Blairgowrie, Perthshire, 21 July 1606. [NRS.RS48.5.133]

ELMSLY, THOMAS, in Tarland, Aberdeenshire, in 1696. [PT]

ELMSLIE, WILLIAM, a servant at Stoniefoord, in the parish of Coull, Aberdeenshire, 1696. [PT]

ERSKINE, JOHN, in New Craig, Glen Isla, Angus, husband of Christian Fell, testament, 1637, Comm. Brechin. [NRS]

ESSIE, JOHN, in Fearn, Angus, 1691. [NRS.E69.11.1]

ETKEN, JOHN, of Major Burnett's Troop of Dragoons, from Aberdeenshire, was mustered at Stirling on 3 December 1697. [FBL.295]

EWART, JAMES, a militiaman in Inchin, Lintrathen, Angus, 1643. [NRS.GD16.50.17.4]

FAIRN, DAVID, in Edzell, Angus, 1691. [NRS.E69.11.1]

FAIRWEATHER, ALEXANDER, a militiaman in Lintrathen, Angus, 1643. [NRS.GD16.50.17.4]

FAIRWEATHER, GEORGE, in Menmuir, Angus, 1691. [NRS.E69.11.1]

FAIRWEATHER, HENRY, a militiaman at Brigend, Lintrathen, Angus, 1643. [NRS.GD16.50.17.4]

FAIRWEATHER, JANET, born 1656, wife of George Mitchell, died in 1736. [Careston, Angus, gravestone]

FAIRWEATHER, ROBERT, in Cortachy and Clova, Angus, 1691. [NRS.E69.11.1]

FALCONER, GEORGE, of the Earl of Airlie's Militia, Angus, 1670. [NRS.GD16.53.39]

FALCONER, JAMES, of the Earl of Airlie's Militia, Angus, 1670. [NRS.GD16.53.39]

FARMER, JOHN, schoolmaster in Dalmunzie, Perthshire, 1685. [DPD.2.97]

FARQUHAR, ALEXANDER, a merchant in Auchenblae, Kincardineshire, a deed in 1696. [NRS.RD4. 79.548]

FARQUHAR, GEORGE, son of James Farquhar in Banchory, Aberdeenshire, was apprenticed to Patrick Murray, s shoemaker in Aberdeen, in 1656. [ACA]

FARQUHAR, GEORGE, son of James Farquhar in Banchory, Aberdeenshire, was apprenticed to Alexander Jaffrey of Kingswells in 1656. [ACA]

FARQUHAR, Sir ROBERT, versus Irvine of Drum, Aberdeenshire, a decreet date 9 February 1654. [NRS.CS98.954]

FARQUHAR, WILLIAM, a shoemaker, with his wife, in Crofts, Glenbuchat, Aberdeenshire, in 1696. [PT]

FARQUHARSON, ALEXANDER, in Inveray, Aberdeenshire, a letter to the Earl of Airlie then in London, dated 24 July 1660. [NRS.GD16.34.179]

FARQUHARSON, ALEXANDER, of Invercauld, Aberdeenshire, a bond of relief dated 1 December 1666, [NRS.GD176.504]; of an Independent Company at Castleton, Braemar in 1674.

FARQUHARSON, ALEXANDER, in Monaltrie, Aberdeenshire, died in 1699. [Crathie gravestone, Aberdeenshire]

FARQUHARSON, CHARLES, of Monaltry near Ballater, Aberdeenshire, a bond of relief, dated 1 December 1666. [NRS.GD176.504]

FARQUHARSON, CHARLES, of Balmoral, Aberdeenshire, a deed in 1696. [NRS.RD3.85.427][PT]; a deed in 1698. [NRS.RD2.81.1.752]

FARQUHARSON, DAVID, of Briochdairg, and his wife Margaret Rattray, a deed, 1640. [NRS.GD16.8.42]

FARQUHARSON, DONALD, of Balfour, Birse, Aberdeenshire, 1667. [AVR]

FARQUHARSON, DONALD, in the Kirkton of Birse, Aberdeenshire, a deed in 1694. [NRS.RD4.74.59]; with lands in Birse, Aboyne, and Migvie, Aberdeenshire, in 1674. [NRS.RH9.3.10]

FARQUHARSON, FINDLAY, the younger of Cults, Aberdeenshire, was accused of the abduction of Elizabetn Morgan, heiress of Torigalter, papers 1700. [NRS.GD124.6.147]

FARQUHARSON, FRANCIS, of Finzean, Birse, Aberdeenshire, 1667. [AVR]; a landowner in the parishes of Birse, Aboyne, and Migvie in 1674. [NRS.RH9.3.10]; deeds in 1698. [NRS.RD4.82.75/354/37]

FARQUHARSON, HARRY, of Bellatrach, Glen Muick, Aberdeenshire, in 1696. [PT]

FARQUHARSON, JAMES, of Colchulston, and William Farquharson of Inverey, Aberdeenshire, Versus John McPherson, brother of Lieutenant Colonel Dugall McPherson of Ballachron, for failing to fulfil the terms of his marriage contract dated 1 April 1652, a letter dated 11 June 1661. [NRS.GD137.3025]

FARQUHARSON, JAMES, of Whitehouse, [brother of Colonel Donald Farquharson of Monaltrie] died in 1666. [Tullich gravestone, Aberdeenshire]

FARQUHARSON, JAMES, of Major Burnett's Troop of Dragoons, from Aberdeenshire, was mustered at Stirling on 3 December 1697. [FBL.295]

FARQUHARSON, JOHN, son of Robert Farquharson, a militiaman in Raverny, Lintrathen, Angus, 1643. [NRS.GD16.50.17.4]

FARQUHARSON, JOHN, of Westoun, Tarland, Aberdeenshire, 1667. [AVR]

FARQUHARSON, JOHN, of Kirkton of Aboyne, Aberdeenshire, 1667. [AVR]

FARQUHARSON, JOHN, of Bellimoire, Aberdeenshire, a bond of relief, dated 1 December 1666. [NRS.GD176.504]

FARQUHARSON, JOHN, of Inverey, Aberdeenshire, of an Independent Company at Castleton, Braemar in 1674; a bond with John Keirie of Gogar, dated 3 September 1694. [NRS.GD124.2.150]

FARQUHARSON, JOHN, was granted the lands of Finegand and the sheiling of Glenbeg, Aberdeenshire, on 21 April 1680. [NRS.GD1.124.4]

FARQUHARSON, JOHN, of Invercauld, Aberdeenshire, a deed in 1698. [NRS.RD4.83.13]

FARQUHARSON, JOHN, born 19 April 1699, son of Lewis Farquharson of Auchindryne, a Catholic priest, died in Balmoral, Aberdeenshire

FARQUHARSON, ROBERT, [1600-1659], husband of Janet Ramsay, parents of John, Robert, Alexander, and three daughters, a militiaman in Raverny, Lintrathen, Angus, 1643. [NRS.GD16.50.17.4] [Farquarson of Ravernie, J. Blair, Dundee, 2003]

FARQUHARSON, ROBERT, of the Kirkton of Birse, Aberdeenshire, a deed, 1692. [NRS.RD4.71.238]

FARQUHARSON, ROBERT, of Broughdarg, Perthshire, a deed in 1696. [NRS.RD3.85.691

FARQUHARSON, THOMAS, of Inveray, Aberdeenshire, a letter to Robert Forbes an advocate in Edinburgh dated 11 May 1693. [NRS.GD112.39.163.13]

FARQUHARSON, WILLIAM, in Broughdearg, Glenshee, Perthshire, a charter witness in 1612. [NRS.GD68.1.143]

FARQUHARSON, WILLIAM, was granted a charter of Finegand in Glenshee, Perthshire, on 17 February 1687. [NRS.GD1.124.9]

FARQUHARSON, WILLIAM, of Brochdarge, was granted Newtoun of Ballatie in the barony of Glen Isla, Angus, on 14 December 1658. [RGS.X.670]

FARQUHARSON, WILLIAM, of Inverey, Aberdeenshire, a bond of relief, dated 1 December 1666. [NRS.GD176.504]; re

parish of Durris, Kincardineshire, 24 July 1660.
[NRS.GD1.38.41]

FEITHIE, KATHERINE, in Alyth, Perthshire, in 1691.
[Hearth Tax Roll] [NRS.E69.19.1]

FELLOW, GEORGE, of Major Burnett's Troop of Dragoons, from Aberdeenshire, was mustered at Stirling on 3 December 1697. [FBL.295]

FENTON, DAVID, of the Earl of Airlie's Militia, Angus, 1670. [NRS.GD16.53.39]

FENTON, DONALD, of the Earl of Airlie's Militia, Angus, 1670. [NRS.GD16.53.39]

FENTON, JAMES, son of Oliver Fenton of Over Ascreavie, Kingoldrum, Angus, married Marion Mason in early 1600s, [NRS.RS33/34]; a bond dated 1658, [NRS.GD16.42.285] [Fenton of Baikie, J. Blair, Dundee, 2006]

FENTON, JAMES, in Lethnot, Angus, militia list, 1643.
[NRS.GD16.50.17.4]

FENTON, JAMES, in Lintrathen, Angus, 1691.
[NRS.E69.11.1]

FENTON, JAMES, in Cortachy and Clova, Angus, 1691.
[NRS.E69.11.1]

FENTON, JAMES, in Kinnaird, Lintrathen, Angus, testament, 1699, Comm. St Andrews. [NRS]

FENTON, JOHN, a militiaman in Craigend, Cortachy, Angus, 1643 [NRS.GD16.50.17.4]

FENTON, JOHN, a militiaman in Inchin, Lintrathen, Angus, 1643. [NRS.GD16.50.17.4]

FENTON, JOHN, in Lintrathen, Angus, 1691.
[NRS.E69.11.1]

FENTON, JOHN, in Cortachy and Clova, Angus, 1691. [NRS.E69.11.1]

FENTON, JOHN, in Bellemenay, Glen Isla, Perthshire, and his wife Janet Frisell, testament, 1662, Comm. Brechin. [NRS]

FENTON, THOMAS, a militiaman at Purgavie, Lintrathan, Angus, 1643. [NRS.GD16.50.17.4]

FENTON, ..., of Ogil, Angus, a Jacobite who fought at the Battle of Killiecrankie, Perthshire, in 1689. [APS.Appendix.ix,159]

FERRIER, A., of the Earl of Airlie's Militia, Angus, 1670. [NRS.GD16.53.39]

FERRIES, or FERGUSON, ALEXANDER, born 1596, graduated from King's College, Aberdeen in 1613, minister at Kindrochat, Aberdeenshire, from 1622 to 1626, then at Crathie, Aberdeenshire, from 1626 to his death in May 1663, husband of Christian Auchterlony, parents of Alexander, John, James, William, and Agnes. [F.6.92]

FINDLATOR, MARGARET, a servant of the laird of Drum, daughter of John Findlator in Burngreen, Methlick, Aberdeenshire, was baptised a Catholic by Father Robert Francis on 29 March 1698, her godfather was John Francis Stewart, the priest's servant. [SNQ.VIII.182]

FINNY, PATRICK, a tenant, with his wife, in Backhillock, Glen Buchat, Aberdeenshire. [1696 Poll Tax]

FERGUSON, ALEXANDER, minister at Braemar, Aberdeenshire, from 1622 to 1626. [F.6.85]

FERGUSON, ALEXANDER, son of John Ferguson the minister in Glen Muick, Aberdeenshire, was apprenticed to Patrick Christie, a merchant in Aberdeen, in 1678. [ACA]

FERGUSON, ALEXANDER, of Dunie in Glenisla, Angus, 1691. [NRS.E69.11.1]

FERGUSON, DONALD, and his wife Marjory Ogilvie, in Auchinlisch, Glen Isla, Angus, testament, 1667, Comm. Brechin. [NRS]

FERGUSON, JOHN, in Cortachy and Clova, Angus, 1691. [NRS.E69.11.1]

FERGUSON, WILLIAM, in Lintrathen, Angus, 1691. [NRS.E69.11.1]

FERRIER, A., of the Earl of Airlie's Militia, Forfarshire, 1670. [NRS.GD16.53.39] minister at Glen Muick, Aberdeenshire, from 1651 until 1681. [F.6.99]

FINDLAY, ALEXANDER, in Navar, Angus, 1691. [NRS.E69.11.1]

FINDLAY, DONALD, tenant in Milton of Inchmarn, Glen Muick, Aberdeenshire, in 1696. [PT]

FINDLAY, JAMES, in Cortachy and Clova, Angus, 1691. [NRS.E69.11.1]

FERGUSON, ROBERT, of Broghdargh, Glen Isla, Angus, testament, 1675, Comm. Brechin. [NRS]

FINDLAY, ANNA, in Tulloch, Glen Isla, Angus, testament, 1625, Comm. Brechin. [NRS]

FINDLOW, JOHN, in French, Glen Isla, Angus, husband of Isobel Clark, testament, 1625, Comm. Brechin. [NRS]

FINLAY, JOHN, a militiaman in Glencallie, Cortachy, Angus, 1643. [NRS.GD16.50.17.4]

FINDLAY, JOHN, in Fearn, Angus, 1691. [NRS.E69.11.1]

FINDLAY, JOHN, in Navar, Angus, 1691. [NRS.E69.11.1]

FISHER, KATHERINE, in Little Dunkeld, Perthshire, in 1691. [Hearth Tax Records] [NRS.E69.19.1]

FLAGER, DUNCAN, and his wife Agnes Bowman, in Kirkton of Lochlee, Angus, testament, 1627, Comm. Brechin. [NRS]

FLEMING, JAMES, in Airlie, Angus, 1691. [NRS.E69.11.1]

FLETCHER, JOHN, in Edzell, Angus, 1691. [NRS.E69.11.1]

FLETCHER, LUDOVICK, of the Earl of Airlie's Militia, Angus, 1670. [NRS.GD16.53.39]

FORBES, ALEXANDER, of Easter Migvie, Aberdeenshire, . [AVR]

FORBES, Sir ARTHUR, of Castle Forbes, Aberdeenshire, a sasine, 18 November 1628, Nova Scotia. [NRS.RS1.25.26]

FORBES, ARTHUR, of Auchintoull, Aberdeenshire, a deed in 1694. [NRS.RD2.77.ii.33]

FORBES, JOHN, of Craigtoun, died in August 1622. [Kearn gravestone, Aberdeenshire]

FORBES, JOHN, born 1643, a minister, died 1708. 'Descended from the Lords of Pitsligo'. [Kincardine O'Neil gravestone, Aberdeenshire]

FORBES, Sir JOHN, of Monimusk, Aberdeenshire, sasines, 1651. [NRS.RS7.5.86/88]

FORBES, Sir JOHN, of Craigievar, Aberdeenshire, deeds, 1693/1694. [NRS.RD4.72; RD2.77ii.33]

FORBES, JOHN, from Kincardineshire, a soldier guarding the Scottish Regalia then in Dunottar Castle from Cromwell's Army from 1651-1652. [DR]

FORBES, Sir JOHN, of Monymusk, Aberdeenshire, the elder, a deed in 1694. [NRS.RD2.78.323]

FORBES, JOHN, a gentleman, and … McIntosh, his wife, in the parish of Crathie, Aberdeenshire, in 1696. [PT]

FORBES, MARJORY, Lady Drum, petitioned for the removal of the laird of Drum, her husband, from the custody of Patrick Leslie of Balquhan,' bigot papist', in 1689. [NRS.GD26.7.762]

FORBES, PATRICK, in Lumquhatt, Aberdeenshire, a deed in 1698. [NRS.RD4.82.1393]

FORBES, THOMAS, MA, minister at Leochel and Cushnie, Aberdeenshire, from 1622 until 1647. [F.VI.135]

FORBES, THOMAS, from Kincardineshire, a soldier guarding the Scottish Regalia then in Dunottar Castle from Cromwell's Army from 1651-1652. [DR]

FORBES, WILLIAM, of Craigievar, Aberdeenshire, a sasine, 22 June 1625. [NRS.RS1.17.252]

FORBES, Sir WILLIAM, of Monymusk, Aberdeenshire, a sasine, Nova Scotia, 4 April 1626. [NRS.RS1.19.166]

FORBES, WILLIAM, from Kincardineshire, a soldier guarding the Scottish Regalia then in Dunottar Castle from Cromwell's Army from 1651-1652. [DR]

FORBES, WILLIAM, of Skellatur, Tarland, Aberdeenshire, 1667. [AVR]

FORBES, WILLIAM, from Kincardineshire, a soldier guarding the Scottish Regalia then in Dunottar Castle from Cromwell's Army from 1651-1652. [DR]

FORBES, WILLIAM, born 1622, died in October 1698, [Strathdon gravestone, Aberdeenshire]

FORDELL, DAVID, in Cortachy and Clova, Angus, 1691. [NRS.E69.11.1]

FORRESTER, ALEXANDER, in Alyth, Perthshire, a charter witness in 1612. [NRS.GD68.1.143]

FORRESTER, DONALD, second son of David Forrester of Easter Rattray, Perthshire, and his wife Elspeth Crichtoun, a bond dated January 1642. [NRS.GD16.1.50]

FORRESTER, JAMES, a militiaman in Cortachy, Angus, 1643. [NRS.GD16.50.17.4]

FORRESTER, JAMES, a militiaman in Tarribuchill, Cortachy, Angus, 1643. [NRS.GD16.50.17.4]

FORRESTER, JAMES, in Lethnott-Lochlee, Angus, 1691. [NRS.E69.11.1]

FORRESTER, NEILL, schoolmaster in Kinloch, Perthshire, 1663, later in Rattray, Perthshire, 1670, husband of Jean Smith. [DPD.2.97]

FORRESTER, THOMAS, a militiaman in Rottuell, Cortachy, Angus, 1643. [NRS.GD16.50.17.4]

FORTOUN, THOMAS, in Airlie, Angus, 1691. [NRS.E69.11.1]

FOULERTON, JOHN, in Airlie, Angus, 1691. [NRS.E69.11.1]

FRAME, AGNES, a servant in the parish of Kindrochit/Braemar, Aberdeenshire, in 1696. [PT]

FRASER, ALEXANDER, of Durris, Kincardineshire, a sasine, 1605. [NRS.RS6.2.118]

FRASER, FRANCIS, born 1649, in Pitmurchie, died 29 April 1718. [Kincardine O'Neil gravestone, Aberdeenshire]

FRASER, JOHN, son of Thomas Fraser of Durris, Kincardineshire, a sasine, 1 July 1603. [NRS.RS6.1.110]

FRASER, ROBERT, in Fearn, Angus, 1691. [NRS.E69.11.1]

FRASER, ROBERT, and his wife Katherine Buchan, at Cant's Mill, Kingoldrum, Angus, testament, 1628, Comm. Brechin. [NRS]

FROST, JOHN, from Kincardineshire, a soldier guarding the Scottish Regalia then in Dunottar Castle from Cromwell's Army from 1651-1652. [DR]

FROSTER, JOHN, in Alyth, Perthshire, in 1691. [Hearth Tax Roll] [NRS.E69.19.1]

FULLERTON, DAVID, a militiaman in Cotter, Kingoldrum, Angus, 1643. [NRS.GD16.50.17.4]

FULLARTON, GEORGE, in Alyth, Perthshire, in 1691. [Hearth Tax Roll] [NRS.E69.19.1]

FULLERTON, JOHN, died on 10 July 16.. aged 78. [Fetteresso gravestone, Kincardineshire]

FUTHIE, DAVID, a militiaman at Purgavie, Lintrathan, Angus, 1643. [NRS.GD16.50.17.4]

FUTHIE, GEORGE, a militiaman in Lintrathen, Angus, 1643. [NRS.GD16.50.17.4]

FUTHIE, JOHN, a militiaman at Campsie, Lintrathen, Angus, 1643. [NRS.GD16.50.17.4]

FUTHIE, ROBERT, son of David Futhie, a militiaman in Pitmidie, Lintrathen, Angus, 1643. [NRS.GD16.50.17.4]

FYFFE, ALEXANDER, in Kincardine O'Neil, Aberdeenshire, a deed in 1696. [NRS.RD4.78.912]

FYFE, ALEXANDER, in Knowhead,Tarland, Aberdeenshire, in 1696. [PT]

FYFFE, DAVID, the younger, in Cortachy, Angus, 1662. [RGS.XI.178]

FYFFE, JOHN, a militiaman in Colzimy, Cortachy, Angus, 1643. [NRS.GD16.50.17.4]

FYFE, JOHN, minister of Navar, Angus, from 1650 to 1658 [F.5.401]

FYFE, JOHN, in Easter Cults,Tarland, Aberdeenshire, in 1696. [PT]

FYFE, JOHN, in Old Kincraig, in Tarland, Aberdeenshire, in 1696. [PT]

FYFE, JOHN, a miller in Bellamore, Glen Muick, Aberdeenshire, in 1696. [PT]

FYFFE, WILLIAM, in Strathmore in the parish of Coull, Aberdeenshire, 1696. [PT]

FYFE, WILLIAM, in Wester Coults, Tarland, Aberdeenshire, in 1696. [PT]

GAY, CHRISTIAN, in Fearn, Angus, 1691. [NRS.E69.11.1]

GAE, WILLIAM, in Cortachy and Clova, Angus, 1691. [NRS.E69.11.1]

GALBRAITH, WILLIAM, of Major Burnett's Troop of Dragoons, from Aberdeenshire, was mustered at Stirling on 10 December 1692. [FBL.295]

GARDYNE, ALEXANDER, of Banchory, Aberdeenshire, a sasine, 1606. [NRS.RS6.2.145]

GARDYNE, ALEXANDER, from Kincardineshire, a soldier guarding the Scottish Regalia then in Dunottar Castle from Cromwell's Army from 1651-1652. [DR]

GARDYNE, ARTHUR, of Banchory, Aberdeenshire, a sasine, 1603. [NRS.RS6.1.110]

GARDYNE, Colonel THOMAS, with his spouse Anne Reland, and their daughter Anne Gardyne, were granted various lands in the Aberdeenshire parishes of Tullich, Glentanar, and Glenmuick, on 30 May 1638. [RA.301]

GARDYNE, JANET, daughter of Arthur Gardyne of Banchory, Aberdeenshire, a sasine, 11 June 1605. [NRS.RS6.2.87]

GARIOCH, ALEXANDER, MA, minister at Cushnie Aberdeenshire, from 1629 until, 1651. [F.VI.137]

GEIKIE, JANET, at the Mill of Craig, Glen Isla, Angus, testament, 1663, Comm. Brechin. [NRS]

GELLIE, CHRISTIAN, servant to the minister in Glen Muick, Aberdeenshire, in 1696. [PT]

GENTLEMAN, JOHN, of the Earl of Airlie's Militia, Angus, 1670. [NRS.GD16.53.39]

GIBB, ROBERT, in Old Town of Lethnot, Angus, husband of Agnes Will, testament, 1688, Comm. Brechin. [NRS]

GIBB, ALEXANDER, in Dykehead of Drumcairn, Lethnot, Angus, husband of Isobel Mair, testament, 1611, Comm. Brechin. [NRS]

GIBB, DAVID, in Lethnott-Lochlee, Angus, 1691. [NRS.E69.11.1]

GIBB, ROBERT, in Navar, Angus, 1691. [NRS.E69.11.1]

GIBB, ROBERT, in Lethnott-Lochlee, Angus, 1691. [NRS.E69.11.1]

GIBB, ROBERT, in Edzell, Angus, 1691. [NRS.E69.11.1]

GIBB, ROBERT, in Lethnott-Lochlee, Angus, 1691. [NRS.E69.11.1]

GIBBON, JAMES, a militiaman at Brigend, Lintrathen, Angus, 1643. [NRS.GD16.50.17.4]

GIBSON, JAMES, in Balntor, a militiaman in Lintrathen, Angus, 1643. [NRS.GD16.50.17.4]

GIBSON, JOHN, a militiaman in Lintrathen, Angus, 1643. [NRS.GD16.50.17.4]

GIBSON, JOHN, of the Earl of Airlie's Militia, Angus, 1670. [NRS.GD16.53.39]

GIBSON, JOHN, in Cortachy and Clova, Angus, 1691. [NRS.E69.11.1]

GIBSON, THOMAS, a militiaman in Lintrathen, Angus, 1643. [NRS.GD16.50.17.4]

GIFFORD, WILLIAM, of Major Burnett's Troop of Dragoons, from Aberdeenshire, was mustered at Stirling on 10 December 1692. [FBL.295]

GILLANDERS, ALASTER, a tenant, with his wife, in Glenbuchat, Aberdeenshire. [1696 Poll Tax]

GILLANDERS, ALEXANDER, in Tilliehardach, in Tarland, Aberdeenshire, in 1696. [PT]

GILLANDERS, MARY, servant to the minister in Glen Muick, Aberdeenshire, in 1696. [PT]

GILLIES, JOHN, born 1681, minister at Careston, Angus, from September 1716 until his death on 1 March 1753. [Careston gravestone]

GLASS, WILLIAM, MA, minister at Cushnie, Aberdeenshire from 1651 until 1666. [F.VI.137]

GLEN, ANDREW, a militiaman in Hill, Lintrathen, Angus, 1643. [NRS.GD16.50.17.4]

GLEN, JANET, in Menmuir, Angus, 1691. [NRS.E69.11.1]

GLENDAY, JAMES, in Airlie, Angus, 1691. [NRS.E69.11.1]

GLENDAY, JOHN, in Muirhouse in Airlie, Angus, 1691. [NRS.E69.11.1]

GLENDEERS, JOHN, in Cortachy and Clova, Angus, 1691. [NRS.E69.11.1]

GOLD, ALEXANDER, in Navar, Angus, 1691. [NRS.E69.11.1]

GOLD, JAMES, and his wife Margaret Strachan, in Drumcairn, Lethnot, Angus, testament, 1614, Comm. Brechin. [NRS]

GOLD, JANET, daughter of the late William Gold, in Cadloch, Lochlee, Angus, testament, 1627, Comm. Brechin. [NRS]

GOLD, ROBERT, and his wife Barbara Smith, in Braco, Navar, Angus, testament, 1683, Comm. Brechin. [NRS]

GOLD, HENRY, in Lethnott-Lochlee, Angus, 1691. [NRS.E69.111]

GORDON, ADAM, dead by 1696, his wife Jean Douglas, their children Adam, Robert, Alexander, Margaret, Helen, and Jacobina, in Glenbuchat, Aberdeenshire, in 1696. [PT]

GORDON, ADAM, of Glenbucket, Aberdeenshire, deeds in 1698. [NRS.RD4.83.37/38/113]

GORDON, ALEXANDER, and WILLIAM, of Abergeldy, a contract with the Earl of Mar re the teinds of Braemar and Easton of Tarland, Aberdeenshire, dated 1616. [NRS.GD33.23.1]

GORDON, ALEXANDER, MA, minister at Glen Muick, Aberdeenshire, from 120 until 1647. [F.6.98]

GORDON, ALEXANDER, of Kincraigie, Tarland, Aberdeenshire, 1667. [AVR]

GORDON, ALEXANDER, of Birsmoir, Birse, Aberdeenshire, 1667. [AVR]

GORDON, ALEXANDER, of the Earl of Airlie's Militia, Angus, 1670. [NRS.GD16.53.39]

GORDON, Lady ELIZABETH, daughter of Charles Gordon, Earl of Aboyne, married Sir John McKenzie the younger of Tarbat, a disposition by Sir George McKenzie of Tarbat, datd 2 January 1685. [NRS.GD305.1.49.5]

GORDON, GEORGE, a tenant, with his wife, in Backhillock, Glen Buchat, Aberdeenshire, in 1696. [PT]

GORDON, GEORGE, at the Mill of Coull, in the parish of Coull, Aberdeenshire, 1696. [PT]

GORDON, ISOBEL, 'a little lass', a servant to Adam Beatty, in Nethertoun, Glenbuchat, Aberdeenshire, in 1696. [PT]

GORDON, JAMES, of Major Burnett's Troop of Dragoons, from Aberdeenshire, was mustered at Stirling on 10 December 1692. [FBL.295]

GORDON, JOHN, of Blelack, Logiemar, Aberdeenshire, 1667. [AVR]

GORDON, JOHN, of Dalquhing, Aboyne, Aberdeenshire, 1667. [AVR]

GORDON, JOHN, of the Earl of Airlie's Militia, Angus, 1670. [NRS.GD16.53.39]

GORDON, JOHN, of Rothiemay, tutor to the Earl of Aboyne, 28 February 1693. [NRS.CS165.613]

GORDON, JOHN, of Kirkton of Glen Buchat, Aberdeenshire, with his wife and daughter Elizabeth, in 1696. [PT]

GORDON, JOHN, of Rothiemay, Aberdeenshire, deeds in 1696. [NRS.RD3. 85.358; RD4.78.875/1031]

GORDON, LUDOVIC, born 1649, graduated MA from King's College in Aberdeen in 1669, minister at Aboyne and Glentanar, Aberdeenshire, from 1679 until his death in October 1694. [F.6.78]; a deed in 1698, [NRS.RD4.82.583]

GORDON, MARJORIE, spouse of Hector Abercrombie of Fetterneir, a sasine, 7 July 1628. [NRS.RS6.176]

GORDON, PATRICK, born 1672, son of Charle Gordon, the Earl of Aboyne, and his wife Elizabeth Lyon, a student at the Scots College at Douai in 1681. [RSC.I.55]

GORDON, ROBERT, in Cortachy and Clova, Angus, 1691. [NRS.E69.11.1]

GORDON, THOMAS, in Kirkton of Clova, Angus, militia list, 1643. [NRS.GD16.50.17.4]

GORDON, WILLIAM, a tenant in Glen Buchat, Aberdeenshire, in 1696. [PT]

GOURLAY, JOHN, and his wife Janet Mill, in Tilliarbit, Navar, Angus, testament, 1681, Comm. Brechin. [NRS]

GOURLAY, N., of the Earl of Airlie's Militia, Angus, 1670. [NRS.GD16.53.39]

GOVE, THOMAS, from Kincardineshire, a soldier guarding the Scottish Regalia then in Dunottar Castle from Cromwell's Army from 1651-1652. [DR]

GOW, ALEXANDER, a tenant, with his wife, in Backhillock, Glen Buchat, Aberdeenshire, in 1696. [PT]

GOW, DONALD, in Little Dunkeld, Perthshire, in 1691. [Hearth Tax Records] [NRS.E69.19.1]

GOW, JAMES, a tenant in Balmoral, in the parish of Crathie, Aberdeenshire, in 1696. [PT]

GOW, JOHN, servant to Adam Beatty, in Nethertoun, Glenbuchat, Aberdeenshire, in 1696. [PT]

GOWRIE, JOHN, born 1658, miller at Bridgend, Angus, died 1716, husband of Euphan McNab, parents of George, Thomas,

Mary, Elizabeth, Katherine, and Jean. [Lintrathen gravestone, Angus]

GRAHAM, JOHN, in Menmuir, Angus, 1691. [NRS.E69.11.1]

GRANT, ALEXANDER, of Ballachastell, of an Independent Company at Strathspey, Aberdeenshire, in 1674

GRANT, JAMES, servant to William Reid in Dulaks, Glenbuchat, Aberdeenshire, in 1696. [PT]

GRANT, JOHN, in Nether Mill of Strathisla, Angus, a deed, 1692. [NRS.RD4.70.385]

GRANTON, THOMAS, of Major Burnett's Troop of Dragoons, from Aberdeenshire, was mustered at Stirling on 10 December 1692. [FBL.295]

GRASSICH, DUNCAN, a sub-tenant in the parish of Crathie, Aberdeenshire, in 1696. [PT]

GRAY, ANDREW, in Kirkton of Clova, Angus, militia list, 1643. [NRS.GD16.50.17.4]

GRAY, JAMES, a militiaman in Cullow, Cortachy, Angus, 1643. [NRS.GD16.50.17.4]

GRAY, JOHN, a militiaman in Airlie, Angus, 1643. [NRS.GD16.50.17.4]

GRAY, JOHN, schoolmaster in Kirkmichael, Perthshire, 1657, and in Moulin, Perthshire, 1667. [DPD.2.97]

GRAY, WILLIAM, of the Earl of Airlie's Militia, Angus, 1670. [NRS.GD16.53.39]

GREIG, ANDREW, ib Burnside of Aislie, Fettercairn, Kincardineshire, a deed,1692. [NRS.RD3.79.177]

GREIVE, FRANCIS, of the Earl of Airlie's Militia, Angus, 1670. [NRS.GD16.53.39]

GRESHICH, JANET, in Little Dunkeld, Perthshire, in 1691. [Hearth Tax Records] [NRS.E69.19.1]

GRESSICH, KATHERINE, in Little Dunkeld, Perthshire, in 1691. [Hearth Tax Records] [NRS.E69.19.1]

GREWAR, CHARLES, in Wester Innerarity, Glen Isla, Angus, husband of Margaret Paterson, testament, 1625, Comm. Brechin. [NRS]

GREWAR, FINDLAY, feuar of Auchtene, parish of Wester Inverarity, and his wife Janet Canzow in the parish of Glen Isla, Angus, testament, 1610, Comm. Brechin. [NRS]

GREWAR, JAMES, a militiaman in Cordache, Lintrathen, Angus, 1643. [NRS.GD16.50.17.4]

GREWAR, JOHN, a militiaman in Inchin, Lintrathen, Angus, 1643. [NRS.GD16.50.17.4]

GRIEG, JOHN, in Fearn, Angus, 1691. [NRS.E69.11.1]

GRIME, JOHN, in Lintrathen, Angus, 1691. [NRS.E69.11.1]

GRIMMAN, MARGARET, in Little Dunkeld, Perthshire, in 1691. [Hearth Tax Records] [NRS.E69.19.1]

GRUGH, GILBERT, schoolmaster in Dunkeld, Perthshire, 1685. [DPD.2.96]

GUTHRIE, DAVID, of Kair, born 1658, son of Harry Guthrie of Halkerton and his wife Margaret Sibbald, graduated MA fron Edinburgh University in 1684, minister at Glen Esk, Angus, from 1687 until his death on 15 November 1697. [F.6.99]

GUTHRIE, GIDEON, MA, minister at Glen Muick, Aberdeenshire, in 1698. [F.6.99]

GUTHRIE, JAMES, schoolmaster in Alyth, Perthshire, 1690. [SHS.4.2]

GUTHRIE, JOHN, of Easter Memus, Angus, a heritable bond, dated 27 November 1680. [NRS.GD16.19.2]

GUTHRIE, PATRICK, schoolmaster in Edzell, Angus, 1690. [SHS.4.2]

GUTHRIE, ROBERT, of the Earl of Airlie's Militia, Angus, 1670. [NRS.GD16.53.39]

HALL, COLIN, in Achinleiss, Glen Isla, Angus, father of Margaret McNicoll, testament, 1633, Comm. Brechin. [NRS]

HALL, COLIN, a militiaman in Hill, Lintrathen, Angus, 1643. [NRS.GD16.50.17.4]

HALL, JOHN, portioner of Easter Inneraritie, Glen Isla, Angus, and his wife Elspeth Rattray, testament, 1614, Comm. Brechin. [NRS]

HALL, JOHN, in Daldakebok, Glen Isla, Angus, husband of Margaret Leslie, testament, 1662, Comm. Brechin. [NRS]

HALL, JOHN, in the barony of Glenisla, Angus, 1663. [RGS.XI.464]

HALL, JOHN, in Glenmarkie, barony of Glen Isla, Angus, 1667. [RGS.XI.1105]

HALL, THOMAS, in Alrick, Glen Isla, Angus, testament, 1668, Comm. Brechin. [NRS]

HALYBURTON, GEORGE, MA, minister of Menmuir Angus, from 1642 to 1644. [F.5.407]

HAMILTON, WILLIAM, from Kincardineshire, a soldier guarding the Scottish Regalia then in Dunottar Castle from Cromwell's Army from 1651-1652. [DR]

HAMPTON, THOMAS, in Lethnott-Lochlee, Angus, 1691. [NRS.E69.11.1]

HANTON, THOMAS, in Lintrathen, Angus, 1691. [NRS.E69.11.1]

HARDIE, JOHN, schoolmaster in Dunkeld, Perthshire, 1668. [DPD.2.96]

HARPER, ANDREW, a servant at the Mill of Coull, in the parish of Coull, Aberdeenshire, 1696. [PT]

HARPER, ELSPET, servant of Harry Farquharson of Bellatrach, Glen Muick, Aberdeenshire, in 1696. [PT]

HAY, JOHN, in Drumcairn, Lethnot, Angus, husband of Margaret Strachan, testament, 1632, Comm. Brechin. [NRS]

HAY, JOHN, of Major Burnett's Troop of Dragoons, from Aberdeenshire, was mustered at Stirling on 10 December 1692. [FBL.295]

HAY, JOHN, a tenant, with his wife, in Uppertoun, Glen Buchat, Aberdeenshire, in 1696. [PT]

HAY, WILLIAM, son of John Hay, with his wife, in Uppertoun, Glen Buchat, Aberdeenshire, in 1696. [PT]

HAY, THOMAS, in Cortachy and Clova, Angus, 1691. [NRS.E69.11.1]

HENDERSON, ANDREW, of Major Burnett's Troop of Dragoons, from Aberdeenshire, was mustered at Stirling on 10 December 1692. [FBL.295]

HENDERSON, GEORGE, in Alyth, Perthshire, a deed, June 1624. [NRS.GD16.12.91]; renounced his claim to land in the barony of Alyth on 9 May 1624, to Lord James Ogilvy. [NRS.GD16.12.41]

HENDERSON, JOHN, in Alyth, Perthshire, in 1691. [Hearth Tax Roll] [NRS.E69.19.1]

HENDERSON, MARK, of Major Burnett's Troop of Dragoons, from Aberdeenshire, was mustered at Stirling on 10 December 1692. [FBL.295]

HENDERSON, PATRICK, of Major Burnett's Troop of Dragoons, from Aberdeenshire, was mustered at Stirling on 10 December 1692. [FBL.295]

HENDERSON, WILLIAM, the elder, in Balbrogie, baillie of John Pearson in Balbrogie, disposed of Balbrogie and Balersho, subscribed in Blairgowrie, Perthshire, on 31 December 1697, also subscribed by Andrew Burman of the Diocese of Dunkeld. [NRS.GD68.1.268]

HENDRIE, DAVID, in Cortachy and Clova, Angus, 1691. [NRS.E69.11.1]

HENRY, JOHN, and his wife Helen Paterson, in Bogside of Tilliearblit, Navar, Angus, testament, 1611, Comm. Brechin. [NRS]

HENRY, THOMAS, in Lethnott-Lochlee, Angus, 1691. [NRS.E69.11.1]

HERALD, JAMES, in Cortachy and Clova, Angus, 1691. [NRS.E69.11.1]

HERALD, JOHN, in Cortachy and Clova, Angus, 1691. [NRS.E69.11.1]

HERRING, DAVID, of Rochquhalloch, a bond, 17 May 1662. [NRS.GD16.3.194]

HERON, WILLIAM, in Lintrathen, Angus, 1691. [NRS.E69.11.1]

HERRIALL, DAVID, in Clova, Angus, militia list, 1643. [NRS.GD16.50.17.4]

HERVIE, ALEXANDER, from Kincardineshire, a soldier guarding the Scottish Regalia then in Dunottar Castle from Cromwell's Army from 1651-1652. [DR]

HETFORD, ROBERT, of Major Burnett's Troop of Dragoons, from Aberdeenshire, was mustered at Stirling on 10 December 1692. [FBL.295]

HEWETT, JOHN, in Edzell, Angus, 1691. [NRS.E69.11.1]

HIGH, JOHN, in Lethnott-Lochlee, Angus, 1691. [NRS.E69.11.1]

HILL, ALEXANDER, in Fearn, Angus, 1691. [NRS.E69.11.1]

HOGG, WILLIAM, from Kincardineshire, a soldier guarding the Scottish Regalia then in Dunottar Castle from Cromwell's Army from 1651-1652. [DR]

HOGG, WILLIAM, in Edzell, Angus, 1691. [NRS.E69.11.1]

HOLBURNE, WILLIAM, Cornet of Major Burnett's Troop of Dragoons, from Aberdeenshire, was mustered at Stirling on 10 December 1692. [FBL.295]

HOOD, ALEXANDER, in Ridd, Airlie, Angus, 1691. [NRS.E69.11.1]

HOOD, JAMES, born 1633, second son of John Hood in Reidie, died 9 March 1673. [Airlie gravestone, Angus]

HOOD, JAMES, schoolmaster in Kirkmichael, Perthshire, 1689. [DPD.2.97]

HOOD, JOHN, born 1607, in Readie, died on 16 January 1669, husband of Janet Irnes. [Airlie gravestone, Angus]

HOPE, WILLIAM, in Lintrathen, Angus, 1691. [NRS.E69.11.1]

HOW, JAMES, in Fermertoun, Fearn, testament, 1705, Comm. Edinburgh. [NRS]

HOWE, JOHN, son of James Howe in Cullen, Banffshire, minister at Birse, Aberdeenshire, from 1698 until his death in 1707. [F.6.83]

HOWIE, THOMAS, a militiaman in Lintrathen, Angus, 1643. [NRS.GD16.50.17.4]

HUMBELL, DAVID, in Navar, Angus, 1691. [NRS.E69.11.1]

HUMELL, AGNES, in Fearn, Angus, 1691. [NRS.E69.11.1]

HUNTER, JOHN, in Airlie, Angus, 1691. [NRS.E69.11.1]

HUTCHIN, JAMES, in Lintrathen, Angus, 1691. [NRS.E69.11.1]

HUTCHEON, JOHN, in Cotton of Airlie, Angus, husband of Janet Malcolm, testament, 1613, Comm. St Andrews. [NRS]

HUTCHEON, JOHN, from Kincardineshire, a soldier guarding the Scottish Regalia then in Dunottar Castle from Cromwell's Army from 1651-1652. [DR]

HUTCHISON, JAMES, in Edzell, Angus, 1691. [NRS.E69.11.1]

HUTTON, JAMES, a militiaman in Hall, Cortachy, Angus, 1643. [NRS.GD16.50.17.4]

INGLIS, ARCHIBALD, of Major Burnett's Troop of Dragoons, Aberdeenshire, was mustered at Stirling on 10 December 1692. [FBL.295]

INGLIS, JOHN, Captain of the Earl of Airlie's Militia, Angus, 1670. [NRS.GD16.53.39]

INNES, ALEXANDER, of Towie, died 18 April 1682. [Migvie gravestone, Aberdeenshire]

INNES, JAMES, of Drumgask, Aboyne, Aberdeenshire, of an Independent Company in 1677.

INNES, JOHN, a militiaman at Brigend, Lintrathen, Angus, 1643. [NRS.GD16.50.17.4]

INNES, WILLIAM, of the Earl of Airlie's Militia, Angus, 1670. [NRS.GD16.53.39]

IRELAND, ANDREW, brother of Thomas Ireland, schoolmaster in Alyth, Perthshire, 1681. [NRS.RD4.49.31 8]

IRELAND, THOMAS, schoolmaster in Alyth, Perthshire, from 1665 until 1678, deeds. [NRS.RD4.14.281; RD2.39.607; RD3.43.386]

IRONS, ALEXANDER, in Fearn, Angus, 1691. [NRS.E69.11.1]

IRONS, JOHN, a militiaman at Brigend, Lintrathen, Angus, in 1643. [NRS.GD16.50.17.4]

IRVINE, ALEXANDER, in Kincraig, in Tarland, Aberdeenshire, in 1696. [PT]

IRVINE, FRANCIS, of Drum, Aberdeenshire, bequethed 16000 merks to the Congragation de propagands fide for the Scottish mission, subscribed in Rome on 3 January 1699. [NRS.CH7.76]

IRVINE, FRANCIS, in Tarland, Aberdeenshire, in 1696. [PT]

IRVINE, JOHN, born 1604, minister of Glenbervie for 44 years, died in 1680, husband of Margaret Gordon. [Glenbervie gravestone, Kincardineshire]

IRVINE, ROBERT, in Pett, in Tarland, Aberdeenshire, in 1696. [PT]

IRVING, ALEXANDER, minister at Birse, Aberdeenshire, from 1593 to 1608. [F.6.82]

IRVIN, Captain ROBERT, of Monboddo, born 1572, died on 6 July 1652. [Fordoun gravestone, Kincardineshire]

JAAP, JOHN, from Kincardineshire, a soldier guarding the Scottish Regalia, then in Dunottar Castle besieged by Cromwell's Army from 1651 to 1652.

JACK, JANET, in Haystoun, Airlie, Angus, testament, 1617, Comm. St Andrews. [NRS]

JAFFRAY, THOMAS, from Kincardineshire, a soldier guarding the Scottish Regalia then in Dunottar Castle from Cromwell's Army from 1651-1652. [DR]

JAMES, JOHN, a militiaman in Lintrathen, Angus, 1643. [NRS.GD16.50.17.4]

JAMIESON, ALEXANDER, from Kincardineshire, a soldier guarding the Scottish Regalia then in Dunottar Castle from Cromwell's Army from 1651-1652. [DR]

JAMIESON, ALEXANDER, in Lethnott-Lochlee, Angus, 1691. [NRS.E69.11.1]

JAMIESON, JEAN, widow of David Ogilvy in Wellton of Creuchie, renounced her life rent in favour of James Ogilvy, brother german to the said David, deed subscribed at Kirkton of Rattray, Perthshire, on 20 July 1618. [BC.166]

JAMIESON, JOHN, from Kincardineshire, a soldier guarding the Scottish Regalia then in unottar Castle from Cromwell's Army from 1651-1652. [DR]

JAMIESON, PATRICK, in Pitnacree, a deed, June 1624. [NRS.GD16.12.91]; renounced his claim to land in the barony of Alyth, Perthshire, on 9 May 1624, to Lord James Ogilvy. [NRS.GD16.12.41]

JAMIESON, THOMAS, in Lethnott-Lochlee, Angus, 1691. [NRS.E69.11.1]

JOHNSTON, JOHN, in Milton in Airlie, Angus, 1691. [NRS.E69.11.1]

JOHNSTONE, WILLIAM, of the Earl of Airlie's Militia, Angus, 1670. [NRS.GD16.53.39]

JOLLY, ALEXANDER, in Menmuir, Angus, 1691. [NRS.E69.11.1]

JOLLIE, DAVID, in Menmuir, Angus, 1691. [NRS.E69.11.1]

JOLLIE, DAVID, in Lethnott-Lochlee, Angus, 1691. [NRS.E69.11.1]

JOLLIE, WILLIAM, in Navar, Angus, 1691. [NRS.E69.11.1]

KANDHEACH, JAMES, in Clova, Angus, militia list, 1643. [NRS.GD16.50.17.4]

KANNO, WILLIAM, in Cortachy and Clova, Angus, 1691. [NRS.E69.11.1]

KEIR, M., of the Earl of Airlie's Militia, Angus, 1670. [NRS.GD16.53.39]

KEIR, MALCOLM, in Little Dunkeld, Perthshire, in 1691. [Hearth Tax Records] [NRS.E69.19.1]

KEITH, ALEXANDER, of Wester Migvie, Aberdeenshire, 1667. [AVR]

KEITH, GEORGE, of Drumtochty, Kincardineshire, a dispute with Sir George Allardyce and John Allardyce of that Ik, on 20 July 1626. [NRS.GD49.128]

KEITH, JOHN, parson of Birse, Aberdeenshire, a lease to Patrick Sandilands of Cotton, dated 12 October 1682. [NRS.GD74.322]

KELLAS, WILLIAM, a tenant, with his wife, in Crofts, Glenbuchat, Aberdeenshire, in 1696. [PT]

KELLIE, ANDREW, in the Cottoun of Turing, Angus, testament, 1649. [NRS.GD188.33.9]

KEMLO, JAMES, the elder and the younger, from Kincardineshire, soldiers guarding the Scottish Regalia, then in Dunottar Castle besieged by Cromwell's Army from 1651 to 1652.

KENDZOW, JAMES, in Claecleugh, Glen Clova, Angus, in 1662. [RGS.XI.178]

KENDO, JOHN, a militiaman in Cotter, Kingoldrum, Angus, 1643. [NRS.GD16.50.17.4]

KENDO, JOHN, in Lintrathen, Angus, 1691. [NRS.E69.11.1]

KENDOW, WILLIAM, in the Holl, Lintrathen, Angus, testament, 1614, Comm. St Andrews. [NRS]

KENDOW, WILLIAM, a militiaman in Holl, Lintrathen, Angus, 1643. [NRS.GD16.50.17.4]

KENOCH, JOHN, in Cortachy and Clova, Angus, 1691. [NRS.E69.11.1]

KENZIACH, JOHN, in Wester Coults, Tarland, Aberdeenshire, in 1696. [PT]

KENZIACH, PATRICK, in Knowhead, Tarland, Aberdeenshire, in 1696. [PT]

KER, WILLIAM, born 1669, in Cotbank, died 23 August 1742, husband of Margaret Strachan, born 1670, died 6 April 1737. [Glenbervie gravestone, Kincardineshire]

KERMACK, THOMAS, a hired lad in Wester Whytside, Angus, 1668. [NRS.CC3.4.6A.762]

KERMOTH, WILLIAM, in Lintrathen, Angus, 1691.
[NRS.E69.11.1]

KEY, DAVID, in Airlie, Angus, 1691. [NRS.E69.11.1]

KIDD, JOHN, a militiaman in Schanelie, Lintrathen, Angus, 1643. [NRS.GD16.50.17.4]

KIDDALS, DAVID, in Lethnott-Lochlee, Angus, 1691.
[NRS.E69.11.1]

KIDDALS, WALTER, in Lethnott-Lochlee, Angus, 1691.
[NRS.E69.11.1]

KILLES, ANDREW, a widower and tenant in Glen Buchat, Aberdeenshire. [1696 Poll Tax]

KILLO, ALEXANDER, from Kincardineshire, a soldier guarding the Scottish Regalia, then in Dunottar Castle besieged by Cromwell's Army from 1651 to 1652.

KING, JAMES, in Cortachy and Clova, Angus, 1691.
[NRS.E69.11.1]

KINNEAR, ALEXANDER, in Edzell, Angus, 1691.
[NRS.E69.11.1]

KINNEAR, JAMES, in Lethnott-Lochlee, Angus, 1691.
[NRS.E69.11.1]

KINNEAR, THOMAS, in Edzell, Angus, 1691.
[NRS.E69.11.1]

KINNINMONTH, WILLIAM, in Hatton of Inverarity, Angus, a bond, 1668. [NRS.CC3.4.6A.762]

LAING, JAMES, in Drumcairn, parish of Lethnot, husband of Anne Gibb, born 1689, died 1737. [Lethnot gravestone, Angus]

LAING, JOHN, baron of Noth, died in March 1634. [Kearn gravestone, Aberdeenshire]

LAIRD, JAMES, a militiaman in Cordache, Lintrathen, Angus, 1643. [NRS.GD16.50.17.4]

LAMB, ANDREW, in Little Dunkeld, Perthshire, in 1691. [Hearth Tax Records] [NRS.E69.19.1]

LAMIE, ANDREW, died 1676, husband of Elspet Anderson, died in 1665. [Edzell gravestone, Angus]

LAMOND, JOHN, of Monidrean and Drum, Aberdeenshire, a list of arms held by him and his tenants in 1686. [NRS.GD1.57.15]

LAUSON, ANDREW, in Lintrathen, Angus, 1691. [NRS.E69.11.1]

LAUSON, JAMES, in Fearn, Angus, 1691. [NRS.E69.11.1]

LAWSON, PATRICK, in Middle Todd, a militiaman in Lintrathen, Angus, 1643. [NRS.GD16.50.17.4]

LAW, THOMAS, in Edzell, Angus, 1691. [NRS.E69.11.1]

LAY, JOHN, a militiaman in Lintrathen, Angus, 1643. [NRS.GD16.50.17.4]

LEASK, JAMES, minister at Braemar, Aberdeenshire, in 1607. [F.6.85]

LEASK, JAMES, probably son of Walter Leask of Leask, minister at Cushnie, Aberdeenshire, from 1608 until 1626. [F.VI.137]

LECKY, ALEXANDER, a militiaman in Kingoldrum, Angus, 1643. [NRS.GD16.50.17.4]

LEIGHTON, THOMAS, in Easter Inneraritie, Glen Isla, Angus, testament, 1621, Comm. Brechin. [NRS]

LEITH, ALEXANDER, of Major Burnett's Troop of Dragoons, from Aberdeenshire, was mustered at Stirling on 10 December 1692. [FBL.295]

LESLIE, JOHN, minister at Birse, Aberdeenshire, in 1611. [F.6.82]

LEITCH, DAVID, in Bracow, Navar, Angus, and his wife Christian Craig, testament, 1613, Comm. Brechin. [NRS]

LESLIE, JOHN, minister at Glen Muick, Aberdeenshire, from 1599 until deposed in 1623. [F.6.82/98]

LESLIE, JOHN, son of George Leslie of Kincraigie and his wife Lucretie Abercrombie, graduated MA from King's College in Aberdeen in 1662, minister at Cushnie, Aberdeenshire, from 1667 until his death in 1671. [F.VI.137]

LETHAM, WALTER, in Middle Todd, a militiaman in Lintrathen, Angus, 1643. [NRS.GD16.50.4]

LEY, WILLIAM, servant of Harry Farquharson of Bellatrach, Glen Muick, Aberdeenshire, in 1696. [PT]

LICHTON, JOHN, in Clova, Angus, a militiaman in 1643. [NRS.GD16.50.17.4]

LIGERTWOOD, JOHN, from Kincardineshire, a soldier guarding the Scottish Regalia then in Dunottar Castle from Cromwell's Army from 1651-1652. [DR]

LIND, JAMES, in Little Dunkeld, Perthshire, in 1691. [Hearth Tax Records] [NRS.E69.19.1]

LINDSAY, ALEXANDER, a militiaman in Arloch, Cortachy, Angus, 1643. [NRS.GD16.50.17.4]

LINDSAY, ALEXANDER, a militiaman in Inglismaquen, Cortachy, Angus, 1643. [NRS.GD16.50.17.4]

LINDSAY, ALEXANDER, graduated MA from King's College, Aberdeen, 1674, minister at Cortachy, Angus, from 1687 to 1690 died 1729, husband of Jean Dall, parents of James, Mary, Elizabeth, and Isobel, testament, 1723, Comm. Brechin. [NRS][F.5.280]

LINDSAY, ALEXANDER, in Cortachy and Clova, Angus, 1691. [NRS.E69.11.1]

LINDSAY, ANDREW, in Clova, Angus, militia list, 1643. [NRS.GD16.50.17.4]

LINDSAY, ANDREW, a militiaman in Balloh, Cortachy, Angus, 1643. [NRS.GD16.50.17.4]

LINDSAY, ANDREW, a militiaman in Cortachy, Angus, 1643. [NRS.GD16.50.17.4]

LINDSAY, ANDREW, in Airlie, Angus, 1691. [NRS.E69.11.1]

LINDSAY, DAVID, in Ballenter in Lintrathen, Angus, 1691. [NRS.E69.11.1]

LINDSAY, DAVID, of Edzell, Angus, and Francis Farquharson of Finzean, a bond over the barony of Glen Esk, dated 23 November 1694. [NRS.GD45.16.1765]

LINDSAY, ANDREW, servant to John Gellie, in Ardow, Lochlee, Angus, testament, 1638, Comm. Brechin. [NRS]

LINDSAY, DAVID, papers, from 1598 until 1611. [NRS.GD1.182.8]

LINDSAY, Sir DAVID, of Edzell, Angus, a tack of lands in the barony of Fearn, Angus, to Alexander Lindsay of Canterland, in 1610. [NRS.GD1.182.3]

LINDSAY, Sir DAVID, of Kinnaird, a tack of the Mains of Easter Edzell, Angus, and of Wester Edzell, date October 1611. [NRS.GD1.182.3]

LINDSAY, DAVID, in Dykehead of Tullo, Cortachy, Angus, testament, 1612, Comm. Brechin. [NRS]

LINDSAY, DAVID, in Lethnot, Angus, militia list, 1643. [NRS.GD16.50.17.4]

LINDSAY, DAVID, a militiaman in Fincreich, Cortachy, Angus, 1643. [NRS.GD16.50.17.4]

LINDSAY, DAVID, a militiaman at Cuthilhill, Lintrathan, Angus, 1643. [NRS.GD16.50.17.4]

LINDSAY, DAVID, of Clova, Angus, a charter, 1662. [RGS.XI.178]

LINDSAY, DAVID, in Kirkton of Clova, Angus, a charter, 1662. [RGS.XI.178]

LINDSAY, DAVID, eldest son of John Lindsay of Edzell, Angus, a marriage contract with Agnes Graham, daughter of

James Graham of Monorgund, dated 1664.
[NRS.GD45.16.1752]; a deed, dated 14 June 1673.
[NRS.GD1.47.211]

LINDSAY, DAVID, of Edzell, Angus, bonds with Alexander and Robert Steill sons of William Steill in Stone of Morphie, dated 10 June 1690. [NRS.GD45.16.1763]

LINDSAY, GEORGE, of Lethnot, Angus, and William Lindsay, baillie of the Regality of Kirriemuir, Angus, subscribed to a bond in 1692. [NRS.GD16.13.125]

LINDSAY, HENRY, a militiaman in Bank, Cortachy, Angus, 1643. [NRS.GD16.50.17.4]

LINDSAY, JAMES, and his wife Bessie Lucas, in Roymantis, Rottual, Angus, testament, 1637, Comm. Brechin. [NRS]

LINDSAY, JAMES, a militiaman in Gleslitt, Cortachy, Angus, 1643. [NRS.GD16.50.17.4]

LINDSAY, JAMES, in Edzell, Angus, 1691. [NRS.E69.11.1]

LINDSAY, JAMES, in Lethnott-Lochlee, Àngus, 1691. [NRS.E69.11.1]

LINDSAY, JAMES, in Cullow, Cortachy, Angus, testament, 1670, Comm. Brechin. [NRS]

LINDSAY, JAMES, in Glenmoy, Angus, wife Isobel Findlay, testament, 1688, Comm. Brechin. [NRS]

LINDSAY, JAMES, in Collone, Cortachy, Angus, testament, 1691, Comm. Brechin. [NRS]

LINDSAY, JEAN, only daughter of Alexander Lindsay of Edzell, Angus, and Walter, Lord Torpichen, a post nuptial marriage contract dated July 1653, they were unable to subscribe to a marriage contract at the time of their marriage in May 1651 as their houses were occupied by soldiers. [NRS.GD119.123]

LINDSAY, JEAN, wife of John Lindsay of Edzell, Angus, a charter of confirmation, 1664. [RGS.XI.628]

LINDSAY, JOHN, of Edzell, Angus, a marriage contract with Jean Carnegie, daughter of Lord Lour, dated 9 August 1647. [NRS.GD1.383.34]

LINDSAY, JOHN, of Edzell, Angus, heir to his uncle David Lindsay of Edzell, in the lands of Wester Edzell in the lordsip of Rescobie, on 12 October 1648. [NRS.GD45.16.1750]

LINDSAY, JOHN, of Edzell, Angus, heir to his father David Lindsay of Edzell, in various properties in the barony of Glen Esk, 1648. [NRS.Retours]; heir to his uncle David Lindsay of the barony of Glen Esk on 26 July 1648. [NRS.GD45.16.1650]

LINDSAY, J., of Edzell, Angus, letters dated 16 July 1667. [NRS.GD16.31.161/162]

LINDSAY, JOHN, in Kirkton of Clova, Angus, a deed, 1625. [NRS.GD16.2.86]

LINDSAY, JOHN, in Kirkton of Clova, Angus, militia list, 1643. [NRS.GD16.50.17.4]

LINDSAY, JOHN, in Edzell, Angus, 1691. [NRS.E69.11.1]

LINDSAY, JOHN, in Cortachy and Clova, Angus, 1691. [NRS.E69.11.1]

LINDSAY, MAGDALENE, daughter of John Lindsay of Edzell, Angus, a marriage contract with Lachlan McIntosh of Torcastle, dated 23 July 1667 – her tocher was 20,000 merks. [NRS.GD176.511]

LINDSAY, ROBERT, in Cortachy and Clova, Angus, 1691. [NRS.E69.11.1]

LINDSAY, ROBERT, in Easter Coul, Lintrathen, Angus, papers 1703-1710. [NRS.GD205.24.148]

LINDSAY, THOMAS, in Cortachy and Clova, Angus, 1691. [NRS.E69.11.1]

LINDSAY, THOMAS, in Fedderege, Angus, and his widow Christian Strachan, testaments, 1610, Comm. Brechin. [NRS]

LINDSAY, THOMAS, in Rochtach, Cortachy, Angus, husband of Margaret Mitchell, testaments, 1624, 1637, Comm. Brechin. [NRS]

LINDSAY, THOMAS, a militiaman in Tarribuchill, Cortachy, Angus, 1643. [NRS.GD16.50.17.4]

LINDSAY, WALTER, in Edzell, Angus, 1691. [NRS.E69.11.1]

LINDSAY, WILLIAM, a militiaman in Newbigging, Cortachy, Angus, 1643. [NRS.GD16.50.17.4]

LINDSAY, WILLIAM, in Cortachy and Clova, Angus, 1691. [NRS.E69.11.1]

LINDSAY, ..., of Edzell, Angus, in 1674. [NRS.CS238.F1.1.1]

LINTON, THOMAS, from Kincardineshire, a soldier guarding the Scottish Regalia then in Dunottar Castle from Cromwell's Army from 1651-1652. [DR]

LISSON, JOHN, a militiaman in Pitmidie, Lintrathen, Angus, 1643. [NRS.GD16.50.17.4]

LITTLEJOHN, PETER, a tradesman at the Mill of Auchterfoull, in the parish of Coull, Aberdeenshire, 1696. [PT]

LIVINGSTONE, JOHN, of Dunlappie, Angus, heir to his father Allan Livingstone of Dunlappie, in the lands of Dunlappy, 1625. [NRS.Retours]

LOUDEN, ALEXANDER, in Lintrathen, Angus, 1691. [NRS.E69.11.1]

LOUDEN, JOHN, in Lintrathen, Angus, 1691. [NRS.E69.11.1]

LOURIE, DAVID, in Edzell, Angus, 1691. [NRS.E69.11.1]

LOUSON, JOHN, in Lethnott-Lochlee, Angus, 1691. [NRS.E69.11.1]

LOW, ALASTER, in Braedownie, Clova, Angus, militia list, 1643. [NRS.GD16.50.17.4]

LOW, ALEXANDER, in Edzell, Angus, 1691. [NRS.E69.11.1]

LOW, ANDREW, in Cortachy and Clova, Angus, 1691. [NRS.E69.11.1]

LOW, DAVID, in Edzell, Angus, 1691. [NRS.E69.11.1]

LOW, DAVID, in Glen Tennet, Lochlee, Angus, husband of Margaret Gold, testament, 1627, Comm. Brechin. [NRS]

LOW, DAVID, in Argeith, Lethnot, Angus, wife Janet Black, testament, 1641, Comm. Brechin. [NRS]

LOW, DAVID, in Sleugleyne, Glenesk, Angus, testament,1671, Comm. Brechin. [NRS]

LOW, DAVID, in Lethnott-Lochlee, Angus, 1691. [NRS.E69.11.1]

LOW, ELSPET, in Edzell, Angus, 1691. [NRS.E69.11.1]

LOW, FINDLAY, in Cortachy and Clova, Angus, 1691. [NRS.E69.11.1]

LOW, JAMES, in Milton of Dalboig, Edzell, Angus, testament, 1617, Comm. St Andrews. [NRS]

LOW, JAMES, in Edzell, Angus, 1691. [NRS.E69.11.1]

LOW, JAMES, of Major Burnett's Troop of Dragoons, from Aberdeenshire, was mustered at Stirling on 10 December 1692. [FBL.295]

LOW, JOHN, and his wife Helen Ross, in Cairncross, Lochlee, Angus, testament 1627, Comm. Brechin. [NRS]

LOW, JOHN, in Kirkton of Clova, Angus, militia list, 1643. [NRS.GD16.50.17.4]

LOW, JOHN, in Menmuir, Angus, 1691. [NRS.E69.11.1]

LOW, JOHN, in Cortachy and Clova, Angus, 1691. [NRS.E69.11.1]

LOW, THOMAS, a militiaman in Cullow, Cortachy, Angus, 1643. [NRS.GD16.50.17.4]

LOW, THOMAS, in Cortachy and Clova, Angus, 1691. [NRS.E69.11.1]

LOW, THOMAS, in Edzell, Angus, 1691. [NRS.E69.11.1]

LOW, WILLIAM, in Glen Tennet, Lochlee, Angus, husband of Margaret Christison, testament, 1627, Comm. Brechin. [NRS]

LOW, WILLIAM, a militiaman in Braeside, Cortachy, Angus, 1643. [NRS.GD16.50.17.4]

LOW, WILLIAM, in Cortachy and Clova, Angus, 1691. [NRS.E69.11.1]

LOWRIE, ARCHBALD, from Kincardineshire, a soldier guarding the Scottish Regalia then in Dunottar Castle from Cromwell's Army from 1651-1652. [DR]

LUCAN, JOHN, a militiaman in Egie, Cortachy, Angus, 1643. [NRS.GD16.50.17.4]

LUCAS, JAMES, a militiaman in Fichill, Cortachy, Angus, 1643. [NRS.GD16.50.17.]

LUCKAS, JAMES, in Cortachy and Clova, Angus, 1691. [NRS.E69.11.1]

LUCAS, JOHN, militiaman in Egie, Cortachy, Angus, 1643. [NRS.GD16.50.17.4]

LUCKAS, JOHN, in Cortachy and Clova, Angus, 1691. [NRS.E69.11.1]

LUCKAS, JOHN DAW, in Cortachy and Clova, Angus, 1691. [NRS.E69.11.1]

LUKE, GEORGE, of Major Burnett's Troop of Dragoons, from Aberdeenshire, was mustered at Stirling on 3 December 1697. [FBL.295]

LUMSDALE, PATRICK, in Menmuir, Angus, 1691. [NRS.E69.11.1]

LUMSDELL, JAMES, in Strathmore in the parish of Coull, Aberdeenshire, 1696. [PT]

LUMSDEN, JAMES, in Easter Clova, Aberdeenshire, a sasine 1626, [NRS.RS1.19.352]

LUMSDEN, JAMES, born 1690, son of William Lumsden in Titaboutie, died in November 1730. [Kildrummy gravestone, Aberdeenshire]

LUNAN, AGNES, born 1608, spouse of James Deuchar, died in 1634. [Airlie gravestone, Angus]

LUNAN, JOHN, in Airlie, Angus, 1691. [NRS.E69.11.1]

LUNDIE, JAMES, at the Kirk of Menmuir, Angus, testament, 1595, Comm. Brechin. [NRS]

LUNDIE, THOMAS, minister at Alyth, Perthshire, husband of Jean Blair, a bond with Lord James Ogilvy, dated August 1632. [NRS.GD16.1.44]; born 1580, minister at Alyth for 34 years, died 8 June 1636, husband of Jane Blair, who died of fever on 26 May 1636. [Alyth gravestone]

LUNNE, ROBERT, in Airlie, Angus, 1691. [NRS.E69.11.1]

LYELL, DAVID, in Cotton of Margie, Lethnot, Angus, husband of Isobel Smart, testament, 1614, Comm. Brechin. [NRS]

LYELL, JAMES, in Fermerton, Fearn, Angus, husband of Elspeth Lindsay testament., 1659, Comm. Brechin. [NRS]

LYELL, JOHN, in Lethnott-Lochlee, Angus, 1691. [NRS.E69.11.1]

LYING, THOMAS, in Edzell, Angus, 1691. [NRS.E69.11.1]

LYON, FREDERICK, minister in Airlie, Angus, 1691. [NRS.E69.11.1]

LYON, JAMES, in Edzell, Angus, 1691. [NRS.E69.11.1]

LYON, JOHN, Major of the Earl of Airlie's Militia, Angus, 1670. [NRS.GD16.53.39]

LYON, PATRICK, in Cardean, Airlie, Angus, testament, 1635, Comm. St Andrews. [NRS]

MCALLESPICK, DUNCAN, in Tanrich in the parish of Kindrochit, Braemar, Aberdeenshire, in 1696. [PT]

MCALLESTER, HECTOR, of Major Burnett's Troop of Dragoons, from Aberdeenshire, was mustered at Stirling on 3 December 1697. [FBL.295]

MCANDREW, JOHN, in Invercauld, in the parish of Kindrochit/Braemar, Aberdeenshire, in 1696. [PT]

MCCOMIE, JOHN, a militiaman in Cordache, Lintrathen, Angus, 1643. [NRS.GD16.50.17.4]

MCCOMIE, MALCOLM, a sub-tenant in the parish of Crathie, Aberdeenshire, in 1696. [PT]

MCDONALD, ALEXANDER, a sub-tenant at Balmoral, in the parish of Crathie, Aberdeenshire, in 1696. [PT]

MCDONALD, DONALD, in Inverey, Aberdeenshire, uncle of Ronald McDonald of Fresatt, a bond dated 12 May 1668. [NRS.GD112.1.612]

MCDONALD, JAMES, of Major Burnett's Troop of Dragoons, from Aberdeenshire, was mustered at Stirling on 3 December 1697. [FBL.295]

MCDOUGALL, JOHN, a sub-tenant in the parish of Crathie, Aberdeenshire, in 1696. [PT]

MCDOUGALL, SAMUEL, a gentleman in Toldor, Glen Muick, Aberdeenshire, in 1696. [PT]

MCEWAN, ALEXANDER, in Auchrenie, Lochlee, Angus, testament,1669, Comm. Brechin. [NRS]

MCEWAN, JAMES, in Little Dunkeld, Perthshire, in 1691. [Hearth Tax Records] [NRS.E69.19.1]

MCFELL, WILLIAM, of Major Burnett's Troop of Dragoons, from Aberdeenshire, was mustered at Stirling on 10 December 1692. [FBL.295]

MCGREGOR, ALEXANDER, in Auchintonell, disposed of all corn, cattle, horses, goods and gear on the lands of Auchintonell, to David Lindsay of Edzell, Angus, on 28 February 1698. [NRS.GD3.14.1.28]

MCGREGOR, ALEXANDER, in Cortachy and Clova, Angus, 1691. [NRS.E69.11.1]

MACGRIGOR, ALEXANDER, in Lethnott-Lochlee, Angus, 1691. [NRS.E69.11.1]

MCGREGOR, alias **GRIERSON, CALLUM,** of Ballater, Aberdeenshire, a bond with John, Earl of Mar, dated 18 October 1700. [GD124.2.165]

MCGREGOR, DAVID, in Navar, Angus, 1691. [NRS.E69.11.1]

MCGREGOR, GEORGE, in Cortachy and Clova, Angus, 1691. [NRS.E69.11.1]

MCGREGOR, JOHN, in Inchgrundell, Lochlee, Angus, testament, 1681, Comm. Brechin. [NRS]

MCGREGOR, JOHN, in Cortachy and Clova, Angus, 1691. [NRS.E69.11.1]

MCGRIGOR, JOHN, a sub-tenant in the parish of Crathie, Aberdeenshire, in 1696. [PT]

MCHARDY, JAMES, a sub-tenant in Balmoral, in the parish of Crathie, Aberdeenshire, in 1696. [PT]

MCHARDY, JOHN, of Daldownie, portioner of Crathie, in the parish of Crathie, Aberdeenshire, in 1696. [PT]

MCINNES, ALEXANDER, a militiaman in Lintrathen, Angus, 1643. [NRS.GD16.50.17.4]

MCINNIS, THOMAS, a militiaman in Raverny, Lintrathen, Angus, 1643. [NRS.GD16.50.17.4]

MCINTAYLOR, JOHN, a sub-tenant in Ellenmore in the parish of Kindrochit/Braemar, Aberdeenshire, in 1696. [PT]

MCINTOSH, ALEXANDER, of Kirkhillock, Glen Isla, Angus, testament,1688, Comm.Brechin. [NRS]

MCINTOSH, alias **BAIN, DONALD,** in Balloch, Glen Isla, Angus, a sasine, 1691. [NRS.RS35.VIII.381]

MCINTOSH, GEORGE, in Blairgowrie, Perthshire, in 1691. [Hearth Tax Roll]

MCINTOSH, LACHLAN, son of Robert McIntosh of Dalmunzie, husband of Janet Ogilvie, a sasine, 1684. [NRS.RS35.VIII.41]

MCINTOSH, LACHLAN, of Torcastle, with the consent of his eldest son and heir Lachland McIntosh, on the one part, and Alexander McPherson of Phonesse, with the consent of his brother Malcolm McPherson, entered a contract of wadset in Ruthven on 21 September 1698. [NRS.GD176.655]

MACINTOSH, RICHARD, in Carrow, Glenshee, Perthshire, reference to in a charter in 1612. [NRS.GD68.1.143]

MCINTOSH, ROBERT, schoolmaster in Kirkmichael, Perthshire, 1673. [DPD.2.97]

MCINTOSH, WILLIAM, of Torcastle, a marriage contract with Margaret Graham, eldest daughter of David Graham of Fintry, dated between 1638 and 1646. [NRS.GD176.368]

MCKAY, DONALD, from Kincardineshire, a soldier guarding the Scottish Regalia then in Dunottar Castle from Cromwell's Army from 1651-1652. [DR]

MACKAY, PETER, born 1670, died 19 April 1742, husband of .....Clark, born 1678, died 12 July 1744. [Kincardine O'Neil gravestone, Aberdeenshire]

MCKENZIE, DONALD, and his wife Janet Campbell, in Dalchalie, Glen Isla, Angus, testament, 1678, Comm. Brechin. [NRS]

MCKENZIE, DUNCAN, a forester at the Castleton of Braemar, Aberdeenshire, in 1677.

MCKENZIE, JOHN, alias McConall Roy, in the Castletoun of Braemar, Aberdeenshire, a deed in 1698. [NRS.RD4.82.149]

MACKIE, ALEXANDER, in the Castletoun of Durris, Aberdeenshire, a sasine, 1604. [NRS.RS6.2.6]

MACKIE, ALEXANDER, in the Glen of Ogilvie, Angus, son of John Mackie there, a sasine, 1638. [NRS.RS34.I.53.]

MACKIE, ALEXANDER, in Lethnott-Lochlee, Angus, 1691. [NRS.E69.11.1]

MACKIE, JOHN, in Lethnott-Lochlee, Angus, 1691. [NRS.E69.11.1]

MACKISON, JAMES, in Fearn, Angus, 1691. [NRS.E69.11.1]

MACKUEL, DUNCAN, in Glenisla, Angus, 1691. [NRS.E69.11.1]

MCLEAN, DONALD DOW, VicConachy, of an Independent Company at Castleton, Braemar, Aberdeenshire, in 1669.

MCLEISH, WILLIAM, born 1682, tenant in Meikle Trochry, Strathbraan, died in 1740. [Little Dunkeld gravestone, Perthshire]

MCLUALD, AGNES, in Ellenmore in the parish of Kindrochit/Braemar, Aberdeenshire, in 1696. [PT]

MCNAB, THOMAS, a merchant in Dunkeld, Perthshire, a deed, 17 January 1636. [NRS.GD1.501.65]

MCNAFF, THOMAS, a shoemaker in Ellenmore in the parish of Kindrochit/Braemar, Aberdeenshire, in 1696. [PT]

MCNICOLL, BEATRIDGE, in Glenisla, Angus, 1691. [NRS.E69.11.1]

MCNICOLL, DONALD, in Glenisla, Angus, 1691. [NRS.E69.11.1]

MCNICOLL, ELSPET, a nurse in Wester Whytside, Angus, 1668. [NRS.CC3.4.6A.762]

MCNICOLL, JAMES, and his wife Catherine Soutar, in Achenrie, Glen Isla, Angus, testament, 1688, Comm. Brechin. [NRS]

MCNICOLL, JAMES, in Glenisla, Angus, 1691. [NRS.E69.11.1]

MACNICOLL, JOHN, in Easter Innerarity, Glen Isla, Angus, husband of Christian Andrew, testament, 1610, Comm. Brechin. [NRS]

MCNICOLL, JOHN, a militiaman at Craigila, Lintrathen, Angus, 1643. [NRS.GD16.50.17.4]

MCNICOLL, JOHN, in Newton, a militiaman in Lintrathen, Angus, 1643. [NRS.GD16.50.17.4]

MCNICOLL, JOHN, portioner of Glenmarkie, Angus, a sasine, 1665. [NRS.RS35.II.163]

MCNICOLL, JOHN, and his wife Margaret Lindsay, in Glenmarkie, Clova, Angus, testament, 1676, Comm. Brechin. [NRS]

MCNICOL, JOHN, in Runtoleave, Prosen, Angus, a deed in 1698. [NRS.RD4.82.1]

MCNICOLL, WILLIAM, portioner of Glen Markie, Glen Isla, Angus, and his wife Christian Clark, testament, 1631, Comm. Brechin. [NRS]

MCNICOLL, WILLIAM, in Easter Inverarity, Glen Isla, Angus, husband of Margaret Grewar, testament, 1664, Comm. Brechin. [NRS]

MCPAUL, JANET, in Little Dunkeld, Perthshire, in 1691. [Hearth Tax Records] [NRS.E69.19.1]

MACQUATIE, ANDREW, in Lintrathen, Angus, 1691. [NRS.E69.11.1]

MCRITCHIE, ..., , a militiaman in Lintrathen, Angus, 1643. [NRS.GD16.50.17.4]

MCROBIE, HARRY, born 1677, died 1766. [Glenbuchet gravestone, Aberdeenshire]

MCRORIE, ALEXADER, a shoemaker in the parish of Crathie, Aberdeenshire, in 1696. [PT]

MCWARKIE, JAMES, a sub-tenant in Ellenmore in the parish of Kindrochit/Braemar, Aberdeenshire, in 1696. [PT]

MCWATTIE, JOHN, a militiaman at Craigila, Lintrathen, Angus, 1643. [NRS.GD16.50.17.4]

MCWILLIAM, JOHN, a servant at the Mill of Coull, in the parish of Coull, Aberdeenshire, 1696. [PT]

MCWILLIE, ROBERT, a servant at Balmoral, in the parish of Crathie, Aberdeenshire, in 1696. [PT]

MADER, ARTHUR, in Bothers, Angus, wife Sarah Peddie, testament, 1609. Comm. Brechin. [NRS]

MADDER, JOHN, in Navar, Angus, 1691. [NRS.E69.11.1]

MAIMES, JOHN, from Kincardineshire, a soldier guarding the Scottish Regalia then in Dunottar Castle from Cromwell's Army from 1651-1652. [DR]

MAIR, DAVID, a militiaman at Campsie, Lintrathen, Angus, 1643. [NRS.GD16.50.17.4]

MAIR, DAVID, in Glenisla, Angus, 1691. [NRS.E69.11.1]

MAIR, GEORGE, a militiaman in Lintrathen, Angus, 1643. [NRS.GD16.50.17.4]

MAIR, JAMES, in Hunthill of Glenesk, Lethnot, Angus, and his wife Katherine Breck, testament, 1624, Comm. Brechin. [NRS]

MALCOLM, ALEXANDER, in Cortachy and Clova, Angus, in 1691. [NRS.E69.11.1]

MALCOLM, ANDREW, in Balgray, Kingoldrum, Angus, testament, 1624, Comm. Brechin. [NRS]

MALCOLM, ANDREW, in Airlie, Angus, 1691. [NRS.E69.11.1]

MALCOLM, JAMES, in Aughter Alyth, Perthshire, formerly in Kilrie, a sasine, 1679. [NRS.RS35.VII.136]

MALCOLM, JAMES, in Airlie, Angus, 1691.
[NRS.E69.11.1]

MALCOLM, ROBERT, in Duny, Glenisla, Angus, a sasine, 1639. [NRS.RS34. I.180]

MALISON, JAMES, in Navar, Angus, 1691. [NRS.E69.11.1]

MAN, JOHN, minister of Lethnot, Angus, in 1589, then at Menmuir, Angus, from 1590 to 1636. [F.5.407]

MARR, GEORGE, in Invercauld in the parish of Kindrochit/Braemar, Aberdeenshire, in 1696. [PT]

MARSHALL, DAVID, a militiaman at Craigila, Lintrathen, Angus, 1643. [NRS.GD16.50.17.4]

MARTIN, ALEXANDER, in Edzell, Angus, 1691.
[NRS.E69.11.1]

MARTIN, ANDREW, in Cotton of Edzell, Angus, testament, 1617, Comm. St Andrews. [NRS]

MARTIN, BESSIE, in Alyth, Perthshire, in 1691. [Hearth Tax Roll] [NRS.E69.19.1]

MARTIN, DAVID, in Edzell, Angus, 1691. [NRS.E69.11.1]

MARTIN, DAVID, in Lethnott-Lochlee, Angus, 1691.
[NRS.E69.11.1]

MASON, JAMES, from Kincardineshire, a soldier guarding the Scottish Regalia then in Dunottar Castle from Cromwell's Army from 1651-1652. [DR]

MASON, WILLIAM, from Kincardineshire, a soldier guarding the Scottish Regalia then in Dunottar Castle from Cromwell's Army from 1651-1652. [DR]

MASSIE, GEORGE, in Knowhead of Cults, Tarland, Aberdeenshire, in 1696. [PT]

MATHER, JOHN, a cotter in Kinruiff, Cortachy, Angus, husband of Isobel Cobb, testament, 1628, Comm. Brechin. [NRS]

MATTHEW, GRISEL, born 1571, spouse of William Malcolm minister at Airlie, died on 23 February 1609. [Airlie gravestone, Angus]

MATHIE, THOMAS, in Easter Glenquharity, Lintrathen, Angus, husband of Marjorie Malcolm, testament, 1618, Comm. St Andrews. [NRS]

MATTERS, GEORGE, in Edzell, Angus, 1691. [NRS.E69.11.1]

MATTERS, JOHN, in Edzell, Angus, 1691. [NRS.E69.11.1]

MATTHEW, JOHN, in Navar, Angus, 1691. [NRS.E69.11.1]

MELDRUM, JAMES, of the Earl of Airlie's Militia, Angus, 1670. [NRS.GD16.53.39]

MELVIL, ALEXANDER, born 1659, died in September 1736, husband of Mary Mc…..born 1659, died 1738, parents of Robert, John, Alexander, and Jean. [Banchory Ternan gravestone, Aberdeenshire]

MENNES, JOHN, from Kincardineshire, a soldier guarding the Scottish Regalia then in Dunottar Castle from Cromwell's Army from 1651-1652.

MENZIES, DUNCAN, schoolmaster in Moulin, Perthshire, 1687. [DPD.2.98]

MERCER, WILLIAM, in Wardfald in the parish of Coull, Aberdeenshire, 1696. [PT]

MERTENE, THOMAS, in Dunkeld, Perthshire, a sasine, 15 June 1603. [NRS.RS48.2.240]

MESSON, JOHN, in Tarland, Aberdeenshire, in 1696. [PT]

MESSON, JOHN, in Easton, Tarland, Aberdeenshire, in 1696. [PT]

MESSON, WILLIAM, in Tarland, Aberdeenshire, in 1696. [PT]

METHIE, JOHN of the Earl of Airlie's Militia, Angus, 1670. [NRS.GD16.53.39]

MICHIE, ALEXANDER, with his wife in Uppertoun, Glen Buchat, Aberdeenshire, in 1696. [PT]

MICHIE, ALEXANDER, born 1688, died 4 May 1743. [Strathdon gravestone, Aberdeenshire]

MICHIE, MARGARET, a servant in the parish of Crathie, Aberdeenshire, in 1696. [PT]

MICKISON, GEORGE, in Edzell, Angus, 1691. [NRS.E69.11.1]

MIDDLETON, GEORGE, in OverBalnastroyne, and his wife Marjory Thomson, a contract with George Gordon, Marquis of Huntly, re various properties in the parish of Glentanar, Aberdeenshire, dated 14 July 1638, witnesses were James Hamilton in Corse, James Hendrie in Roberstoun, and Patrick Anderson, James Anderson, and Alexander Bruce were the notaries. [RA.308]

MILL, ALEXANDER, in Lethnott-Lochlee, Angus, 1691. [NRS.E69.11.1] 67. [AVR]

MIDDLETON, JOHN, in Woodfield, in the parish of Coull, Aberdeenshire, 1696. [PT]

MIDDLETON, ROBERT, the proctor in Lord Ogilvie's house, Cortachy, Angus, militia list, 1643. [NRS.GD16.50.17.4]

MILL, ALEXANDER, in Cortachy and Clova, Angus, 1691. [NRS.E69.11.1]

MILL, DAVID, in Lethnott-Lochlee, Angus, 1691. [NRS.E69.11.1]

MILL, ISABEL, in Lethnott-Lochlee, Angus, 1691. [NRS.E69.11.1]

MILL, JOHN, in Fearn, Angus, 1691. [NRS.E69.11.1]

MILL, JOHN, in Cortachy and Clova, Angus, 1691. [NRS.E69.11.1]

MILL, THOMAS, in Fearn, Angus, 1691. [NRS.E69.11.1]

MILL, THOMAS, in Glen Isla, Angus, testament, 1662, Comm. Brechin. [NRS]

MILLAR, ALEXANDER, in Cammock, Glen Isla, Angus, husband of Jean Laiky, testament, 1599, Comm. Brechin. [NRS]

MILLAR, ALISTER a militiaman in Hill, Lintrathen, Angus, 1643. [NRS.GD16.50.17.4]

MILLAR, JANET, in Little Dunkeld, Perthshire, in 1691. [Hearth Tax Records] [NRS.E69.19.1]

MILLAR, JOHN, a militiaman in Lintrathen, Angus, 1643. [NRS.GD16.50.17.4]

MILLAR, ROBERT, a hired man at Wester Whytside, Angus, 1668. [NRS.CC3.4.6A.762]

MILLER, WILLIAM, in Dunkeld, Perthshire, a sasine, 4 June 1608. [NRS.RS48.6.465]

MILNE, ALEXANDER, in Achronie, Lochlee, Angus, husband of Katherine Duncan, testament, 1627 Comm. Brechin. [NRS]

MILNE, ANDREW, minister of Fetteresso, 1605-1640. [Fetteresso gravestone, Kincardineshire]

MYLNE, ANDREW, from Kincardineshire, a soldier guarding the Scottish Regalia then in Dunottar Castle from Cromwell's Army from 1651-1652. [DR]

MYLNE, GEORGE, Colonel of the Earl of Airlie's Militia, Angus, 1670. [NRS.GD16.53.39]

MILNE, JAMES, in Tilliearblit, Navar, Angus, husband of Isobel Davidson, testament, 1630, Comm. Brechin. [NRS]

MILNE, JAMES, a militiaman in Cotgibber, Cortachy, Angus, 1643. [NRS.GD16.50.17.4]

MILNE, JAMES, a militiaman in Airlie, Angus, 1643. [NRS.GD16.50.17.4]

MILNE, JOHN, the younger, in Middle Todd, a militiaman in Lintrathen, Angus, 1643. [NRS.GD16.50.17.4]

MILNE, JOHN, in Auchronie, Lochlee, Angus, testament, 1627, Comm. Brechin. [NRS]

MILNE, JOHN, servant to David, Earl of Ogilvy, in the Kirkton of Cortachy, Angus, a deed, 29August 1702. [NRS.GD16.2.110]

MILNE, PATRICK, a militiaman in Airlie, Angus, 1643. [NRS.GD16.50.17.4]

MILNE, ROBERT, a tenant, with his wife, in Milltown of Glen Buchat, Aberdeenshire, in 1696. [PT]

MYLNE, WILLIAM, a militiaman at Kinnaird, Lintrathen, Angus, 1643. [NRS.GD16.50.17.4]

MITCHELL, ALEXANDER, a militiaman in Cortachy, Angus, 1643. [NRS.GD16.50.17.4]

MITCHELL, ALEXANDER, a militiaman in Cordachy, Lintrathen, Angus, 1643. [NRS.GD16.50.17.4]

MITCHELL, ALEXANDER, and his wife Isobel Burne in Bukood of Cortachy, Angus, testament, 1688, Comm. Brechin. [NRS]

MITCHELL, ALEXANDER, in Navar, Angus, 1691. [NRS.E69.11.1]

MITCHELL, ANDREW, in Edzell, Angus, 1691. [NRS.E69.11.1]

MITCHELL, GEORGE, husband of Janet Fairweather, born 1656, died 1736, [Careston gravestone, Angus]

MITCHELL, JAMES, in Lintrathen, Angus, 1691. [NRS.E69.11.1]

MITCHELL, JAMES, in Cortachy and Clova, Angus, 1691. [NRS.E69.11.1]

MITCHELL, JAMES, a cottar in the parish of Crathie, Aberdeenshire, in 1696. [PT]

MITCHELL, JANET, servant to John Gordon of Kirkton of Glen Buchat, Aberdeenshire. [1696 Poll Tax]

MITCHELL, JOHN, in Milton of Glen Isla, husband of Christian Spalding, testament, 1610, Comm. Brechin. [NRS]

MITCHELL, JOHN, a militiaman in Lintrathen, Angus, 1643. [NRS.GD16.50.17.4]

MITCHELL, JOHN, in Cortachy and Clova, Angus, 1691. [NRS.E69.11.1]

MITCHELL, PATRICK, a militiaman at Craigila, Lintrathen, Angus, 1643. [NRS.GD16.50.17.4]

MITCHELL, THOMAS, in Clova, Angus, militia list, 1643. [NRS.GD16.50.17.4]

MITCHELL, THOMAS, a militiaman in Lintrathen, Angus, 1643. [NRS.GD16.50.17.4]

MITCHELL, THOMAS, and his wife Catherine Grewar, in Wester Innerarity, Glen Isla, Angus, testament, 1662, Comm. Brechin. [NRS]

MITCHELL, THOMAS, in Cortachy and Clova, Angus, 1691. [NRS.E69.11.1]

MITCHELL, WALTER, in Lethnott-Lochlee, Angus, 1691. [NRS.E69.11.1]

MITCHELL, WILLIAM, in Strathcathro, husband of Margaret Leg, testament, 1627, Comm. Brechin. [NRS]

MITCHELL, WILLIAM, in Fearn, Angus, 1691. [NRS.E69.11.1]

MITCHELL, WILLIAM, a weaver, with his wife, in Crofts, Glenbuchat, Aberdeenshire. [1696 Poll Tax]

MOFFATT, JOHN, from Kincardineshire, a soldier guarding the Scottish Regalia then in Dunottar Castle from Cromwell's Army from 1651-1652. [DR]

MOINTON, ROBERT, in Bush, Clova, Angus, militia list, 1643. [NRS.GD16.50.17.4]

MOIR, ADAM, a tenant, with his wife, in Badenyon, Glenbuchat, Aberdeenshire. [1696 Poll Tax]

MOIR, JOHN, a tenant, with his wife, in Badenyon, Glenbuchat, Aberdeenshire. [1696 Poll Tax]

MOIR, JOHN, a tenant, with his wife, in Uppertoun, Glenbuchat, Aberdeenshire. [1696 Poll Tax]

MOIR, MARGARET, in the parish of Kindrochit, Aberdeenshire, in 1696. [PT]

MOIR, WILLIAM, a tenant, with his wife, in Uppertoun, Glen Buchat, Aberdeenshire, 1696. [PT]

MOLISON, ANDREW, in Edzell, Angus, 1691. [NRS.E69.11.1]

MOLISON, JOHN, in Edzell, Angus, 1691. [NRS.E69.11.1]

MONCREIFF, JOHN, in Blairgowrie, Perthshire, in 1691. [Hearth Tax Roll] [NRS.E69.19.1]

MOOR, ROBERT, sr., of Major Burnett's Troop of Dragoons, from Aberdeenshire, was mustered at Stirling on 3 December 1697. [FBL.295]

MOOR, ROBERT, jr of Major Burnett's Troop of Dragoons, from Aberdeenshire, was mustered at Stirling on 3 December 1697. [FBL.295]

MOREIS, ALEXANDER, son of Thomas Moreis a malt-man burgess of Aberdeen, educated at Marischal College, Aberdeen, in 1665, schoolmaster in Fettercairn, Kincardineshire. [MCA.II.230]

MORES, DAVID, in Fearn, Angus, 1691. [NRS.E69.11.1]

MORES, DAVID, born 1616, died on 5 May 1696, husband of Isobel Mitchell, born 1620, died 7 March 1694, parents of Elizabeth Mores. [Fettercairn gravestone, Kincardineshire]

MOREIS, JOHN, from Kincardineshire, a soldier guarding the Scottish Regalia then in Dunottar Castle from Cromwell's Army from 1651-1652. [DR]

MOREIS, ROBERT, from Kincardineshire, a soldier guarding the Scottish Regalia then in Dunottar Castle from Cromwell's Army from 1651-1652. [DR]

MORGAN, ALEXANDER, a tenant, with his wife, in Backhillock, Glen Buchat, Aberdeenshire. [1696 Poll Tax]

MORGAN, JAMES, a servant at the Mains of Auchterfoull, in the parish of Coull, Aberdeenshire, 1696. [PT]

MORICE, JOHN, a tenant in Achnacraig, Glen Muick, Aberdeenshire, in 1696. [PT]

MORTIE, JOHN, a militiaman in Cotter, Kingoldrum, Angus, 1643. [NRS.GD16.50.17.4]

MORTON, DAVID, in Fearn, Angus, 1691. [NRS.E69.11.1]

MOWAT, THOMAS, from Kincardineshire, a soldier guarding the Scottish Regalia then in Dunottar Castle from Cromwell's Army from 1651-1652. [DR]

MOYINES, JAMES, a militiaman in Tarribuchill, Cortachy, Angus, 1643. [NRS.GD16.50.17.4]

MOYT, THOMAS, a militiaman in Pitmidie, Lintrathen, Angus, 1643. [NRS.GD16.50.17.4]

MUCKETT, FRANCIS, in Edzell, Angus, 1691. [NRS.E69.11.1]

MURRAY, ALEXANDER, from Kincardineshire, a soldier guarding the Scottish Regalia then in Dunottar Castle from Cromwell's Army from 1651-1652. [DR]

MURRAY, CHARLES, of Major Burnett's Troop of Dragoons, from Aberdeenshire, was mustered at Stirling on 3 December 1697. [FBL.295]

MURRAY, DAVID, in Burnhead of Auchranney, Glen Isla, Angus, testament, 1667, Comm. Brechin. [NRS]

MURRAY, JAMES, son of James Murray in Sheltie of Strachan, Kincardineshire, was apprenticed to John Ross a merchant in Aberdeen in 1651. [ACA]

MURRAY, JAMES, a servant of John, Earl of Atholl, Perthshire, a bond, 1670. [NRS.B59.38.6.19]

MUSHET, GEORGE, of the Earl of Airlie's Militia, Angus, 1670. [NRS.GD16.53.39]

MUSTARD, JOHN, born 1676, in Lethendy, Perthshire, died on 2 January 1731, husband of Helen Brodie, born 1687, died in October 1760. [Lethendy gravestone]

MUSTARD, THOMAS, born 1643, in Cookstoun, died 22 August 1675, husband of Margaret Watson. [Airlie gravestone, Angus]

MYELL, JAMES, in Cortachy and Clova, Angus, 1691. [NRS.E69.11.1]

MYELL, THOMAS, in Cortachy and Clova, Angus, 1691. [NRS.E69.11.1]

MYLNE, ALEXANDER, from Kincardineshire, a soldier guarding the Scottish Regalia then in Dunottar Castle from Cromwell's Army from 1651-1652. [DR]

NAIRNE, JOHN, in Coatmore in the parish of Coull, Aberdeenshire, 1696. [PT]

NEILL, ALEXANDER, a militiaman in Schanelie, Lintrathen, Angus, 1643. [NRS.GD16.50.17.4]

NEILL, DAVID, a militiaman at Campsie, Lintrathen, Angus, 1643. [NRS.GD16.50.17.4]

NEISH, JOHN, in the Mansion of Navar, Angus, testament, 1658, Comm. Brechin. [NRS]

NEWTON, ALEXANDER, husband of Elspet Adam born in 1677, died in Clintley 1701. [Lintrathen gravestone, Angus]

NICOLL, ALEXANDER, in Airlie, Angus, 1691. [NRS.E69.11.1]

NICOLL, DAVID, in Menmuir, Angus, 1691. [NRS.E69.11.1]

NICOLL, FRANCIS, in Lethnott-Lochlee, Angus, 1691. [NRS.E69.11.1]

NICOLL, HENRY, in Lethnott-Lochlee, Angus, 1691. [NRS.E69.11.1]

NICOLL, ISABEL, in Edzell, Angus, 1691. [NRS.E69.11.1]

NICOLL, JAMES, in Clunie in Glenisla, Angus, 1691. [NRS.E69.11.1]

NICOLL, JOHN, a militiaman in Holl, Cortachy, Angus, 1643. [NRS.GD16.50.17.4]

NICOLL, JOHN, in Airlie, Angus, 1691. [NRS.E69.11.1]

NICOLL, JOHN, in Lethnott-Lochlee, Angus, 1691. [NRS.E69.11.1]

NICOLL, JOHN, in Cannok, Glen Isla, Angus, husband of Janet Alexander, testament, 1629, Comm. Brechin. [NAS]

NICOL, JOHN, in Cambock, Glen Isla, Angus, testament, 1667, Comm. Brechin. [NRS]

NICOL, WILLIAM, son of John Nicol in Lenros, died on 25 April 1673. [Airlie gravestone, Angus]

NICOLL, WILLIAM, in Airlie, Angus, 1691. [NRS.E69.11.1]

NICOLL, WILLIAM, in Lintrathen, Angus, 1691. [NRS.E69.11.1]

NICOLL, WILLIAM, in Lethnott-Lochlee, Angus, 1691. [NRS.E69.11.1]

NICOLSON, CATHERINE, widow of Alexander Grant of Abergeldie, Aberdeenshire,1666. [RGS.XI.991]

NORIE, ROBERT, graduated MA from St Andrews in 1630, minister of Lethnot, Angus, from 1639 to 1684. [F.5.399]

NORIE, ROBERT, graduated MA from St Andrews 1596, minister at Fearn, Angus, in 1607, then at Strathcathro, Angus, from 1610 to 1643, husband of Bessie Donaldson. [F.5.417]

OCHTERLONY, DAVID, son of David Ochterlony the minister at Fordoun, Kincardineshire, was apprenticed to Charles Dune, a merchant in Aberdeen in 1678. [ACA]

OFFICER, JAMES, born 1684, tenant of the Mains of Dillivard, died 12 April 1752. [Glenbervie gravestone, Kincardineshire]

OGILVY, ALEXANDER, a militiaman in Colziny, Cortachy, Angus, 1643. [NRS.GD16.50.17.4]

OGILVIE, ALEXANDER, a militiaman in Tarribuchill, Cortachy, Angus, 1643. [NRS.GD16.50.17.4]

OGILVIE, ALEXANDER, a militiaman in Balpath, Cortachy, Angus, 1643. [NRS.GD16.50.17.4]

OGILVIE, ALEXANDER, a militiaman in Cordachy, Lintrathen, Angus, 1643. [NRS.GD16.50.17.4]

OGILVIE, ALEXANDER, a militiaman in Lintrathen, Angus, 1643. [NRS.GD16.50.17.4]

OGILVIE, ALEXANDER, and his wife Isobel Findlay, in Glenmoy, testament, 1658, Comm. Brechin. [NRS]

OGILVY, ALEXANDER, of the Earl of Airlie's Militia, Angus, 1670. [NRS.GD16.53.39]

OGILVIE, ALEXANDER, of Pooll in Lintrathen, Angus, 1691. [NRS.E69.11.1]

OGILVIE, ALEXANDER, of Old Allen in Lintrathen, Angus, 1691. [NRS.E69.11.1]

OGILVIE, ANDREW, and his wife Janet Findlay, in Fichell, Cortachy, Angus, testament, 1624, Comm. Brechin. [NRS]

OGILVIE, ANDREW, in Lintrathen, Angus, 1691.
[NRS.E69.11.1]

OGILVIE, ANDREW, in Newton of Lintrathen, Angus, 1691.
[NRS.E69.11.1]

OGILVY, ANDREW, spouse of Janet Gibson, died 12 November 16... aged 74. [Lintrathen gravestone, Angus]

OGILVIE, ANDREW, in Cortachy and Clova, Angus, 1691.
[NRS.E69.11.1]

OGILVIE, COLIN, son of David Ogilvie of Newton, Angus,1651. [NRS.RS34.3.382]

OGILVIE, DAVID, of Bellity, Glen Isla, Angus, born 1560, died1620, husband of Janet McNicoll, parents of David, James, Donald, Isobel, testament, 1621, Comm. Brechin.
[NRS.CC3.3.4.115] [Ogilvy of Newton of Bellaty in Glenisla, J. Blair, Dundee, 2009]

OGILVY, DAVID, of Bellaty, 1585-1658, husband of Magdalen Ogilvy daughter of John Ogilvy of Powrie, parents of Thomas, George, David, Marjory, and Janet. [Ogilvy of Newton of Bellaty in Glenisla, J. Blair, Dundee, 2009]; David Ogilvy of Bellatie, Glen Shee, Perthshire, a referred to in a charter in 1612. [NRS.GD68.1.143]

OGILVY, DAVID, of Pearsie, a charter of lands in Glen Markie, Glen Shee, Perthshire, dated in 1612.
[NRS.GD68.1.143]

OGILVIE, DAVID, of Glaswell, heir to his father David Ogilvie of Glasswell, in the lands of Kirkhillocks, barony of Glen Isla, Angus, 1631. [NRS.Retours; Forfar]

OGILVIE, DAVID, of Newton, Glen Isla, Angus, his widow Margaret Campbell, testament 1602, Comm. Brechin. [NRS]

OGILVY, DAVID, of Newtoun, heir to his father James Ogilvy of Newtoun, in a quarter of the lands of Glen Markie with its windmill, in the barony of Glen Isla, Angus, 1636.
[NRS.Retours][NRS.GD68.1.188]

OGILVIE, DAVID, and wife Grissell Lichtoun, in Ficheill, Angus, testament 1637, Comm. Brechin. [NRS]

OGILVY, Sir DAVID, in Lord Ogilvie's house, Cortachy, Angus, militia list, 1643. [NRS.GD16.50.17.4]

OGILVIE, DAVID, of Clova, Angus, militia list, 1643. [NRS.GD16.50.17.4]

OGILVIE, DAVID, in Auldallan, a militiaman in Lintrathen, Angus, 1643. [NRS.GD16.50.17.4]

OGILVIE, DAVID, son of Thomas Ogilvie of Persie, a militiaman in Lintrathen, Angus, 1643. [NRS.GD16.50.17.4]

OGILVIE, DAVID, in Kinnaltie, of the Earl of Airlie's Militia, Angus, 1670. [NRS.GD16.53.39]

OGILVIE, Sir DAVID, of Clova, Angus, born1616, and died in1681, versus Sir John Keith of Pexoburne, for payment of 4,000 merks dued under a bond dated 10 June1665, on 3 June 1674, [NRS.GD16.41.556]; a bond, 23 November 1671, [NRS.GD16.2.111]; testament 1688, his relict Isobel Guthrie, testament, 1698, Comm. Brechin. [NRS][Ogilvy of Clova, J. Blair, Dundee, 2006]

OGILVIE, Sir DAVID, of Innerquharity, Angus, and Margaret Erkine, daughter of Sir John Erskine of Dun, a marriage contract, 1662. [NRS.GD205.Box 12, bundle 33]

OGILVY, DAVID, of the Earl of Airlie's Militia, Angus, 1670. [NRS.GD16.53.39]

OGILVIE, Sir DAVID, of Clova, Angus, writs, 1688. [NRS.CS229.0.1.1]; served in Airlie's Troop in 1667, a Lieutenant of an Independent Horse Troop in 1674, a Jacobite at the Battle of Killiecrankie, Perthshire, in 1689. [APS, Appendex ix.54]; a deed in 1698. [NRS.RD2.81.1.576]

OGILVIE, DAVID, in Edzell, Angus, 1691. [NRS.E69.11.1]

OGILVIE, DAVID, in Fearn, Angus, 1691. [NRS.E69.11.1]

OGILVIE, DAVID, in Cortachy and Clova, Angus, 1691. [NRS.E69.11.1]

OGILVIE, DAVID, in Airlie, Angus, 1691. [NRS.E69.11.1]

OGILVIE, DAVID, of Peattie, was educated at the University of St Andrews -MA in 1669, minister of Birse, Aberdeenshire, from 1685 until 1697, deeds in 1696 and 1698, died in December 1714. [F.6.83] [NRS.RD2.77ii.464; RD4.83.949]

OGILVIE, DAVID, in Lintrathen, Angus, 1691. [NRS.E69.11.1]

OGILVIE, DAVID, in Alyth, Perthshire, in 1691. [Hearth Tax Roll] [NRS.E69.19.1]

OGILVIE, DAVID, of Over Kinaltie, Angus, a bond with James, the Earl of Airlie, and Lord James Ogilvie, dated 5 January 1692. [NRS.GD16.42.278]

OGILVIE, DONALD, a militiaman in Cullow, Cortachy, Angus, 1643. [NRS.GD16.50.17.4]

OGILVIE, EUPHAME, JANET, MARGARET, and MARY, heirs portioner to their father Robert Ogilvie of Bellachie, in lands of Glen Markie, barony of Glen Isla, Angus, 1605. [NRS.Retours]

OGILVIE, GEORGE, a militiaman in Airlie, Angus, 1643. [NRS.GD16.50.17.4]

OGILVIE, GEORGE, of Fornethy, a militiaman in Lintrathen, Angus, 1643. [NRS.GD16.50.17.4]

OGILVIE, Lieutenant GEORGE, of Barras, Kincardineshire, a soldier guarding the Scottish Regalia then in Dunottar Castle from Cromwell's Army from 1651-1652.

OGILVY, GEORGE, Corporal of the Earl of Airlie's Militia, Angus, 1670. [NRS.GD16.53.39]

OGILVY, GEORGE, of the Earl of Airlie's Militia, Angus, 1670. [NRS.GD16.53.39]

OGILVY, GEORGE, son of David Ogilvy of Newton, Angus, 1666. [NRS.RD4.51.32; GD68.1.232]

OGILVIE, GEORGE, tutor and brother of the laird of Innerqharritie, Angus, and Jean Ogilvie his wife, a deed, 1692. [NRS.RD4.7.1157]

OGILVY, ISOBEL, relict of Thomas Fenton in Coul, and her sons James and William, a bond, 1668. [NRS.CC3.4.6A.762]

OGILVY, ISOBEL, an overmaid in Wester Whytside, Angus, 1668. [NRS.CC3.4.6A.762]

OGILVY, JAMES, of Balfour, Kingoldrum, Angus, born around 1563, and his wife Helen Clephane, marriage contract dated 22 October 1579, [NRS.GD121/2.box 8.1]; parents of James, John, Gilbert, Patrick, and Jean; testament, 1613, Comm. Brechin. [NRS][Ogilvy of Balfour, J. Blair, Dundee, 2008]

OGILVIE, JAMES, of Newton, Angus, heir to his father John Ogilvie of Newton, in a quarter of the lands of Glen Markie, in the barony of Glen Markie, 1629. [NRS.Retours]

OGILVIE, JAMES, of Inshewan, Angus, born1635-died1724, husband of Jean, daughter of Walter Stewart of Cluny, marriage contract dated 4 July 1664, [NRS.GD16.44.27], parents of John, James, Elizabeth, and possibly Catherine and Jean. [Ogilvy of Inshewan, J. Blair, Dundee, 2010]

OGILVIE, JAMES, of Shannellie, Lintrathen, a militiaman in Angus, 1643. [NRS.GD16.50.17.4]

OGILVIE, JAMES, in Lord Ogilvie's house, Cortachy, Angus, militia list, 1643. [NRS.GD16.50.17.4]

OGILVIE, JAMES, a militiaman in Airlie, Angus, 1643. [NRS.GD16.50.17.4]

OGILVIE, JAMES, a militiaman in Tarribuchill, Cortachy, Angus, 1643. [NRS.GD16.50.17.4]

OGILVIE, JAMES, a militiaman in Lintrathen, Angus, 1643. [NRS.GD16.50.17.4]

OGILVIE, JAMES, fiar of Newton in Glen Isla, Angus, a bond with James Farquharson in Lednathie, dated 6 July 1657. [NRS.GD16.8.44]; of Newton of Glenisla, a bond and tack, 27 September 1662. [NRS.RD3.5.255]

OGILVIE, JAMES, in Shank of Glenmoy, Angus, testament 1661, Comm. Brechin. [NRS]

OGILVY, JAMES, Captain of the Earl of Airlie's Militia, Angus, 1670. [NRS.GD16.53.39]

OGILVY, JAMES, a baillie, of the Earl of Airlie's Militia, Angus 1670. [NRS.GD16.53.39]

OGILVY, JAMES, of the Earl of Airlie's Militia, Angus, 1670. [NRS.GD16.53.39]

OGILVY, JAMES, in Raggall, of the Earl of Airlie's Militia, Angus, 1670. [NRS.GD16.53.39]

OGILVY, JAMES, in Cortachy, of the Earl of Airlie's Militia, Angus, 1670. [NRS.GD16.53.39]

OGILVIE, JAMES, in Fettercairn, Kincardineshire, a letter to William Black, an advocate in Aberdeen, dated17 August 1691. [NRS.GD406.1.3741]

OGILVIE, JAMES, in Lintrathen, Angus, 1691. [NRS.E69.11.1]

OGILVIE, JAMES, a bailie of Alyth, Perthshire, a deed in 1698. [NRS.RD3.90.353]

OGILVY, JOHN, of Inshewan, Angus, born1590 - died 1663, husband of Jane, daughter of Patrick Ogilvy of Muirton, parents of James, Patrick, David, Elizabeth, Isabella, and possibly John. [Ogilvy of Inshewan, J. Blair, Dundee, 2010]

OGILVY, JOHN, of Newton of Glenisla, Angus, a charter witness in 1612. [NRS.GD68.1.143]

OGILVY, JOHN, of Inverquharity, Angus, heir to his father Sir John Lindsay of Inverquharity, in the lands of Wester Glenquharities and Ballintoir, in the barony of Lintrathen, 1618. [NRS.Retours]; a note of his rentals from his lands in Kirriemuir, Angus, in 1619. [NRS.GD205.22.39]

OGILVY, JOHN, of Bello, husband of Annabel Spalding, disposed of half the lands of Bello to Patrick Ogilvy of Bendochy, a charter in the 1620s. [NRS.GD16.12.261]

OGILVY, JOHN, of Braesides, Cortachy, Angus, testaments, 1626, 1630, Comm. Brechin. [NRS]

OGILVIE, Sir JOHN, of Innerquharitie, Angus, a sasine, 23 July 1627, Nova Scotia. [NRS.RS1.22.9]

OGILVIE, JOHN, of Peil, a wadsetter, a militiaman in Lintrathen, Angus, 1643. [NRS.GD16.50.17.4]

OGILVIE, JOHN, of Peill, a Corporal of the Earl of Airlie's Militia, Angus, 1670. [NRS.GD16.53.39]

OGILVY, JOHN, a militiaman in Rottuell, Cortachy, Angus, 1643. [NRS.GD16.50.17.4]

OGILVY, JOHN, a militiaman in Glencallie, Cortachy, Angus, 1643. [NRS.GD16.50.17.4]

OGILVIE, JOHN, a militiaman at Castlehill, Lintrathan, Angus, 1643. [NRS.GD16.50.17.4]

OGILVIE, JOHN, a militiaman in Lintrathen, Angus, 1643. [NRS.GD16.50.17.4]

OGILVY, JOHN, a militiaman in Cotter, Kingoldrum, Angus, 1643. [NRS.GD16.50.17.4]

OGILVY, JOHN, a servant, a militiaman in Lintrathen, Angus, 1643. [NRS.GD16.50.17.4]

OGILVY, JOHN, in Glenmoy, Cortachy, Angus, testament, 1650, Comm. Brechin. [NRS]

OGILVY, Captain JOHN, of Wester Whytside, Angus, died 1667, husband of Janet Fenton, parents of William, Thomas, Charles, Elizabeth, and Isobel, testament, 1668. [NRS.CC3.4.6A.762]

OGILVY, JOHN, in Newton, of the Earl of Airlie's Militia, Angus, 1670. [NRS.GD16.53.39]

OGILVY, JOHN, of the Earl of Airlie's Militia, Angus, 1670. [NRS.GD16.53.39]

OGILVIE, JOHN, in Alyth, Perthshire, was granted a charter subscribed in Alyth on 4 April 1674 of the lands of Shealwalls, Wester Bogside, to James Ramsay, fiar of Bamff. [BC.303]

OGILVY, JOHN, of Balfour, Angus, testament, 1697, Comm. Brechin. [NRS]

OGILVIE, Sir JOHN, of Innerquharity, Angus, and Margaret Ogilvy, eldest daughter of James Ogilvy of Cluney, a marriage contract, 1697. [NRS.GD205.Box 12, bundle 33]; a deed in 1698. [NRS.RD4.82.501]

OGILVY, JOHN, of Inshewan, Angus, born 1590, died 1663, husband of Jane Ogilvy, daughter of Patrick Ogilvy of Muitton, parents of James, Patrick, David, Elizabeth, Isabella, John. [NRS.RS35.8.133][NRS.GD16.41.694]

OGILVIE, JOHN, a militiaman in Kinloch, Lintrathen, Angus, 1643. [NRS.GD16.50.17.4]

OGILVIE, JOHN, the younger of Balntor, a militiaman in Lintrathen, Angus, 1643. [NRS.GD16.50.17.4]

OGILVIE, JOHN, of Peill, a Corporal of the Earl of Airlie's Militia, Angus, 1670. [NRS.GD16.53.39]

OGILVY, JOHN, in Burnside of Alyth, Perthshire, assignation of a bond, in 1670. [NRS.GD205.box 22, 102]

OGILVIE, JOHN, in Blackstoun in Airlie, Angus, 1691. [NRS.E69.11.1]

OGILVIE, JOHN, of Bruside in Cortachy and Clova, Angus, 1691. [NRS.E69.11.1]

OGILVIE, JOHN, in Cortachy and Clova, Angus, 1691. [NRS.E69.11.1]

OGILVIE, JOHN, in Lintrathen, Angus, 1691. [NRS.E69.11.1]

OGILVIE, JOHN, in Airlie, Angus, 1691. [NRS.E69.11.1]

OGILVY, LUDOVIC, of the Earl of Airlie's Militia, Angus, 1670. [NRS.GD16.53.39]

OGILVIE, PATRICK, a militiaman at Brigend, Lintrathen, Angus, 1643. [NRS.GD16.50.17.4]

OGILVY, PATRICK, of the Earl of Airlie's Militia, Angus, 1670. [NRS.GD16.53.39]

OGILVIE, ROBERT, portioner of Bellatie, Glen Shee, Perthshire, a referred to in a charter in 1612. [NRS.GD68.1.143]

OGILVIE, ROBERT, of the Earl of Airlie's Militia, Angus, 1670. [NRS.GD16.53.39],

OGILVY, THOMAS, of Inshewan, Angus, born 1565, died 1601, married Barbara Lyon, daughter of James Lyon of Glenogil in 1587, she died 1593, parents of John, Helen, and Rebecca, [RGS.VI.195][NRAS.C14][NRS.Comm.Ed.9.1.1596]

OGILVY, Sir THOMAS, of Lintrathen, Angus, husband of Sir Patrick Ruthven, 1634. [NRS.GD16.34.12]

OGILVIE, THOMAS, youngest son of the deceased James Ogilvie of Cuthilhill, a bond 17 May 1662. [NRS.GD16.3.194]

OGILVY, THOMAS, in Ledenhendrie, 1678. [NRS.GD16.8.21]

OGILVY, THOMAS, of Bellaty, Angus, born1620 – died 1695], a bond, 1668. [NRS.CC3.4.6A.762]; of Bellatie in Glenisla, Angus, 169,1. [NRS.E69.11.1]; in 1700. [NRS.GD1.931.29; SC47.56.7.1]; husband of [1] Anna Ramsay, parents of Thomas and Magdalene, [2] ?, parents of Margaret. [Ogilvy of Newton of Bellatly in Glenisla, J. Blair, Dundee, 2009]

OGILVIE, THOMAS, of Persie, a militiaman in Lintrathen, Angus, 1643. [NRS.GD16.50.17.4]

OGILVY, THOMAS, of the Earl of Airlie's Militia, Angus, 1670. [NRS.GD16.53.39]

OGILVIE, THOMAS, in Cordack in Lintrathen, Angus, 1691. [NRS.E69.11.1]

OGILVIE, THOMAS, in Lintrathen, Angus, 1691. [NRS.E69.11.1]

OGILVIE, THOMAS, in Cortachy and Clova, Angus, 1691. [NRS.E69.11.1]

OGILVY, WILLIAM, a militiaman in Cotter, Kingoldrum, Angus, 1643. [NRS.GD16.50.17.4]

OGILVY, WILLIAM, the younger, a militiaman in Cotter, Kingoldrum, Angus, 1643. [NRS.GD16.50.17.4]

OGILVY, WILLIAM, of the Earl of Airlie's Militia, Angus, 1670. [NRS.GD16.53.39]

OGILVIE, WILLIAM, in Lord Ogilvie's house, Cortachy, Angus, militia list, 1643. [NRS.GD16.50.17.4]

OGILVIE, WILLIAM, in Alyth, Perthshire, in 1691. [Hearth Tax Roll] [NRS.E69.19.1]

OLIVER, DAVID, in Glen Isla, Angus, testament, 1642, Comm. Brechin. [NRS]

OLIVER, THOMAS, at West Mill of Glen Isla, Angus, husband of Janet Ogilvie, testament, 1662, Comm. Brechin. [NRS]

ORD, JOHN, born 1644 in Cullen, Banffshire, graduated MA from King's College in Aberdeen in 1668, minister at Cluny, Aberdeenshire, from 1685 until his death in 1700. [F.6.87]

ORME, DAVID, minister at Monimail, Aberdeenshire, a deed in 1698. [NRS.RD4.83.1361]

PAIN, JOHN, a militiaman in Cotter, Kingoldrum, Angus, 1643. [NRS.GD16.50.17.4]

PATERSON, ELSPET, in Menmuir, Angus, 1691. [NRS.E69.11.1]

PATERSON, WILLIAM, from Kincardineshire, a soldier guarding the Scottish Regalia, then in Dunottar Castle besieged by Cromwell's Army from 1651 to 1652.

PATON, ANDREW, in Dykehead of Cortachy, Angus, a bond, 29 August 1702. [NRS.GD16.2.110]

PATON, JOHN, and his wife Christian Fyffe, in Cotterton of Kilrie Glen Isla, Angus, testament, 1612, Comm. Brechin. [NRS]

PEDDIE, ALEXANDER, [1], a militiaman at New Mylne, Lintrathen, Angus, 1643. [NRS.GD16.50.17.4]

PEDDIE, ALEXANDER, [2], a militiaman at New Mylne, Lintrathen, Angus, 1643. [NRS.GD16.50.17.4]

PEDDY, JAMES, in Kirklandbank of Alyth, Perthshire, a deed, June 1624. [NRS.GD16.12.91]; renounced his claim to land in the barony of Alyth on 9 May 1624, to Lord James Ogilvy. [NRS.GD16.12.41]

PEDDIE, JAMES, a militiaman in Raverny, Lintrathen, Angus, 1643. [NRS.GD16.50.17.4]

PEDDIE, JAMES, a militiaman at Kinnaird, Lintrathen, Angus, 1643. [NRS.GD16.50.17.4]

PEDDIE, JOHN, a militiaman at New Mylne, Lintrathen, Angus, 1643. [NRS.GD16.50.17.4]

PHILIP, JOHN, a ploughman in Wester Whytside, Angus, 1668. [NRS.CC3.4.6A.762]

PHILLIP, THOMAS, in Cortachy and Clova, Angus, 1691. [NRS.E69.11.1]

PHILP, GEORGE, a militiaman in Kingoldrum, Angus, 1643. [NRS.GD16.50.17.4]

PHILP, JOHN, a militiaman in Airlie, Angus, 1643. [NRS.GD16.50.17.4]

PHILP, THOMAS, in Cortachy, Angus, husband of Margaret Wollum died 1616. [Cortachy gravestone]

PHINN, JAMES, the cook in Lord Ogilvie's house, Cortachy, Angus, militia list, 1643. [NRS.GD16.50.17.4]

PIGGOTT, ALEXANDER, in Kirriemuir, Angus, was witness to a charter in November 1607. [NRS.GD68.1.129]

PIGOTT, ALEXANDER, in Lintrathen, Angus, 1691. [NRS.E69.11.1]

PIGGOT, JOHN, graduated MA from King's College, Aberdeen, 1608, schoolmaster of Tannadice, Angus, minister of Lochlee, Angus, from 1622 to 1637, then at Cortachy, Angus, from 1637 until his death in 1657. [F.5.280/399]

PIGGOT, JOHN, in Westerton, a militiaman in Lintrathen, Angus, 1643. [NRS.GD16.50.17.4]

PILLMOR, WILLIAM, in Blairgowrie, Perthshire, in 1691. [Hearth Tax Roll] [NRS.E69.19.1]

PIPER, GEORGE, in Lethnott-Lochlee, Angus, 1691. [NRS.E69.11.1]

PITCAITHLY, JOHN, in Burnside of Duncrub, 16 October 1686. [NRS.GD56.91]

PITSCOTTIE, JAMES, of Major Burnett's Troop of Dragoons, from Aberdeenshire, was mustered at Stirling on 10 December 1692. [FBL.295]

POLL, THOMAS, tailor at Westhill of Dunlappie, Angus, testament, 1602, Comm. Brechin. [NRS]

PORTER, JAMES, in Fearn, Angus, 1691. [NRS.E69.11.1]

POUTIE, JAMES, MA, minister at Cushnie, Aberdeenshire, in 1628. [F.VI.137]

POWIE, THOMAS, a militiaman in Lintrathen, Angus, 1643. [NRS.GD16.50.17.4]

PRESSAN, JOHN, in Burnside of Achnarie, Glen Isla, Angus, testament, 1613, Comm. Brechin. [NRS]

PRINGLE, CHRISTINE, in Little Dunkeld, Perthshire, in 1691. [Hearth Tax Records] [NRS.E69.19.1]

PRINGLE, WILLIAM, a Sergeant of Major Burnett's Troop of Dragoons, from Aberdeenshire, was mustered at Stirling on 10 December 1692. [FBL.295]

PROCTOR, ALEXANDER, in Galey, Cortachy, Angus, testament 1656, Comm. Brechin. [NRS],

PROCTOR, JAMES, a militiaman in Murskreichys, Cortachy, Angus, 1643. [NRS.GD16.50.17.4]

PROCTOR, JANET, daughter of the late John Proctor, in Fetteregie, Angus, testament, 1681, Comm. Brechin. [NRS]

PROVOST, JOHN, a tenant, with his wife, in Uppertoun, Glen Buchat, Aberdeenshire, in 1696. [PT]

QUEE, JOHN, from Tilleamont, Tyre, Aberdeenshire, died at sea aboard the George, probate 1678, PCC. [TNA]

RAE, JOSHUA, minister at Cortachy, Angus, testament 1629, relict Margaret Collace, Comm. Brechin. [NRS]

RAINY, ARTHUR, a weaver, with his wife, in Milltown of Glen Buchat, Aberdeenshire in1696. [PT]

RAMSAY, ALEXANDER, in Alyth, Perthshire, a bond dated August 1632. [NRS.GD16.1.44]

RAMSAY, ALEXANDER, in the Mill of Innerquiech, Angus, a bond dated August 1632. [NRS.GD16.1.44]

RAMSAY, ALEXANDER, in Kirkton of Clova, Angus, militia list, 1643. [NRS.GD16.50.17.4]

RAMSAY, ALEXANDER, of the Earl of Airlie's Militia, Angus, 1670. [NRS.GD16.53.39]

RAMSAY, DAVID, graduated MA from St Andrews in 1612, minister of Cortachy, Angus, from 1628, died in 1637, husband of Christian Scrymgeour, parents of Patrick etc. [F.5.280]

RAMSAY, DAVID, a militiaman in Lintrathen, Angus, 1643. [NRS.GD16.50.17.4]

RAMSAY, DAVID, of the Earl of Airlie's Militia, Angus, 1670. [NRS.GD16.53.39]

RAMSAY, GILBERT, of Bamff, Perthshire, sold part of Little Bamff to Thomas Mackie, his wife and sons, on 7 January 1631. [BC.199][NRS.GD83]

RAMSAY, GILBERT, a Jacobite, was killed at the Battle of Killiecrankie, Perthshire, in 1689. [APS.Appendix, ix.163]

RAMSAY, JAMES, in Bahood, Clova, Angus, militia list, 1643. [NRS.GD16.50.17.4]

RAMSAY, JAMES, born 1586, died 3 June 1646. [Inverarity gravestone, Angus]

RAMSAY, JOHN, of Wester Ogill, Angus, a disposition, 1650. [BrMS.2/1.1/8]

RAMSAY, JAMES, of the Earl of Airlie's Militia, Angus, 1670. [NRS.GD16.53.39]

RAMSAY, JAMES, schoolmaster in Tannadice, Angus, 1690. [SHS.4.2]

RAMSAY, JAMES, minister of Cortachy, Angus, from 1697 to 1700. [F.5.280]

RAMSAY, JOHN, in Auldallan, a wadsetter and militiaman in Lintrathen, Angus, 1643. [NRS.GD16.50.17.4]

RAMSAY, MARGARET, daughter of Gilbert Ramsay of Bamff in Perthshire, and David Ramsay of Jordanstone, Angus, a marriage contract subscribed in Alyth on 24 April 1657. [BC.257]

RAMSAY, WILLIAM, son of David Ramsay in Grantully, Perthshire, versus John Stewart of Arntullie, on 21 November 1656. [NRS.GD38.1.206]

RAMSAY, JOHN, in Alyth, Perthshire, in 1691. [Hearth Tax Roll] [NRS.E69.19.1]

RAMSAY, WILLIAM, in Alyth, Perthshire, in 1691. [Hearth Tax Roll] [NRS.E69.19.1]

RANEY, JOHN, from Kincardineshire, a soldier guarding the Scottish Regalia then in Dunottar Castle from Cromwell's Army from 1651-1652. [DR]

RATTRAY, ALEXANDER, fiar of Dalrizean, Perthshire, Janet Hering his wife, and their son Andrew Rattray, a charter following a marriage contract with John Lyon of Cossins and his daughter Elspeth Lyon, re the land and sheiling in Glenbeg, Dalrizeane, dated 30 April 1643. [NRS.GD16.24.161]

RATTRAY, JAMES, schoolmaster of Rattray, Perthshire, 1639. [DPD.2.98]

RATTRAY, JAMES, a militiaman in Pitmidie, Lintrathen, Angus, 1643. [NRS.GD16.50.17.4]

RATTRAY, JAMES, of Rannaguillan, part owner of Camboik in Glen Isla, Angus, an inventory, 1700. [NRS.GD1.931.29]; sold the lands of Camboik in Glen Isla to Thomas Ogilvie of Bellaty on 13 May 1700. [NRS.GD1.932.29]

RATTRAY, JOHN, in Balquhome, a deed, June 1624. [NRS.GD16.12.91]; a bond dated August 1632. [NRS.GD16.1.44]

RATTRAY, JOHN, minister at Rattray, Perthshire, and his wife Margaret Ramsay, a bond, May 1630. [NRS.GD16.1.40]

RATTRAY, JOHN, minister at Ruthven, versus John Garden of Lawtoun re 5,000 merks due under a bond, 10 November 1679. [NRS.GD16.41.595]

RATTRAY, PATRICK, in Kirktoun of Rattray, Perthshire, a sasine, 5 February 1607. [NRS.RS48.5.373]

RATTRAY, SYLVESTER, of Persie, Angus, and his wife Marie Stewart, letters of reversion re te lands of Arntullie to Captain Ramsay on 28 September 1609. [NRS.GD1.446.55]

RAVER, JOHN, a tenant, with his wife, in Backhillock, Glen Buchat, Aberdeenshire, in 1696. [PT]

RAY, JOSEPH, born 1593, son of Reverend Thomas Ray, graduated MA from St Andrews in 1611, minister of Cortachy, Angus, from 1620 to 1628, husband of Margaret Collace, parents of John and Annas. [F.5.279]

RAY, THOMAS, minister of Cortachy, Angus, from 1582 to 1618. [F.5.279]

REATH, ALEXANDER, of Major Burnett's Troop of Dragoons, from Aberdeenshire, was mustered at Stirling on 10 December 1692. [FBL.295]

REID, ALEXANDER, son of James Reid and his wife Isabel Meldrum in Banchory Ternan, Aberdeenshire, a physician to King Charles I, a prolific writer on medical subjects, died in October 1641. [F.6.79]

REID, ALEXANDER, in Menmuir, Angus, 1691. [NRS.E69.11.1]

READ, ALEXANDER, born 1604, sometime in Doune of Strathardle, Perthshire, died in 1671, husband of Mary Hendry. [Kirkmichael gravestone, Perhshire]

REID, JAMES, in Cortachy and Clova, Angus, 1691. [NRS.E69.11.1]

REID, JAMES, in Tarland, Aberdeenshire, in 1696. [PT]

RID, JOHN, 1686. [Airlie gravestone, Angus]

REID, JOHN, son and heir of John Reid of Haltoun of Creuchy, a sasine to his faher's lands, subscribed at Scone, Perthshire, on 6 December 1614. [BC.157][NRS.GD83]

REID, JOHN, born 1632, smith, died 1702, wife Margaret Hood. [Fearn gravestone, Angus]

REID, JOHN, from Kincardineshire, a soldier guarding the Scottish Regalia then in Dunottar Castle from Cromwell's Army from 1651-1652. [DR]

REID, ROBERT, son of James Reid of Mid Clova, Aberdeenshire, a sasine, 25 May 1627. [NRS.RS1.21.192]

REID, ROBERT, son of James Reid and Isabel Meldrum in Pitfoddels, graduated MA from King's College in Aberdeen in 1600, minister at Banchory Ternan, Aberdeenshire, from 1602 until after 1643. [F.6.80]

REID, ROBERT, from Kincardineshire, a soldier guarding the Scottish Regalia then in Dunottar Castle from Cromwell's Army from 1651-1652. [DR]

REID, ROBERT, son of John Reid of Birnes and his wife Margaret Paton, was educated at Marischal College in Aberdeen from 1651 until 1655, minister at Banchory Ternan, Aberdeenshire, from 1662 until 1682. [F.6.80]

REID, ROBERT, in Migvie, Aberdeenshire, 1667. [AVR]

REID, THOMAS, son of James Reid and his wife Isabel Meldrum in Banchory Ternan, Aberdeenshire, graduated MA from Marischal College in Aberdeen in 1600 and MA from Oxford in 1620, Latin Secretary to King James VI, a metaphysician and Latin poet, founder of the first public reference library in Scotland, died in 1624. [F.6.79]

REID, WALTER, a militiaman in Balnakilie, Lintrathen, Angus, 1643. [NRS.GD16.50.17.4]

REID, WILLIAM, in Sithill, Cortachy, Angus, husband of Catherine Young, testament, 1661, Comm. Brechin. [NRS]

REID, WILLIAM, a tenant, with his wife, in Dulaks, Glenbuchat, Aberdeenshire, in 1696. [PT]

RHIND, JOHN, from Kincardineshire, a soldier guarding the Scottish Regalia then in Dunottar Castle from Cromwell's Army from 1651-1652. [DR]

RIACH, JOHN, a tenant in Head of Inch, Glen Muick, Aberdeenshire, in 1696. [PT]

RIACH, WILLIAM, in Belnacraig in the parish of Coull, Aberdeenshire, 1696. [PT]

RICHARD, JAMES, in Navar, Angus, 1691. [NRS.E69.11.1]

RICHARDSON, ANTHONY, of Major Burnett's Troop of Dragoons, from Aberdeenshire, was mustered at Stirling on 10 December 1692. [FBL.295]

RICHARDSON, ARCHIBALD, of Major Burnett's Troop of Dragoons, from Aberdeenshire, was mustered at Stirling on 10 December 1692. [FBL.295]

RICHARDSON, JAMES, in Navar, Angus, 1691. [NRS.E69.11.1]

RICHARDSON, JOHN, and his wife Elspet Ramsay, in Inneraritie, Glen Isla, Angus, testament, 1612, Comm. Brechin. [NRS]

RICHARDSON, JOHN, in Fearn, Angus, 1691.
[NRS.E69.11.1]

RITCHIE, DAVID, in Old Kincraig, in Tarland, Aberdeenshire, in 1696. [PT]

RITCHIE, JOHN, in Blacklunan in Glenisla, Angus, 1691. [NRS.E69.11.1]

RITCHIE, JOHN, in Fearn, Angus, 1691. [NRS.E69.11.1]

RITCHIE, JOHN, a gardener in Invercauld, in the parish of Kindrochit/Braemar, Aberdeenshire, in 1696. [PT]

RITCHIE, THOMAS, a militiaman at Brigend, Lintrathen, Angus, 1643. [NRS.GD16.50.17.4]

ROBB, HENRY, in Clova, Angus, militia list, 1643. [NRS.GD16.50.17.4]

ROBB, JAMES, a militiaman in Holl, Cortachy, Angus, 1643. [NRS.GD16.50.17.4]

ROBB, JAMES, in Craiginvitie, Glen Isla, Angus, husband of Elspet Hunter, testament, 1662, Comm. Brechin. [NRS]

ROBB, JOHN, cotter in Craigmale, Glen Isla, Angus, testament, 1629, Comm. Brechin. [NRS]

ROBE, JAMES, in Cortachy and Clova, Angus, 1691. [NRS.E69.11.1]

ROBBIE, DAVID, and his wife Elspet Robb, in Eglismachen, Cortachy, Angus, testament, 1637, Comm. Brechin. [NRS]

ROBBIE, DAVID, and his wife Margaret Edward, in Fetteregie, Cortachy, Angus, testament, 1637, Comm. Brechin. [NRS]

ROBERTSON, AGNES, in Dun of Glen Isla, Angus, testament, 1610, Comm. Brechin. [NRS]

ROBERTSON, ALASTER, in Gobintore, Glen Isla, Angus, testament, 1675, Comm. Brechin. [NRS]

ROBERTSON, ALEXANDER, minister of Aboyne and Glentanar, Aberdeenshire, in 1612. [F.6.79]

ROBERTSON, ALEXANDER, was educated at Marischal College in Aberdeen from 1619 until 1623, minister at Cluny, Aberdeenshire, from 1623 until 1653, died after 1659. [F.6.87]

ROBERTSON, ALEXANDER, in Clova, Angus, militia list, 1643. [NRS.GD16.50.17.4]

ROBERTSON, ALEXANDER, of Struan, Perthshire, a bond, 12 May 1662. [NRS.RD2/5.68]

ROBERTSON or NILSON, ALEXANDER, in Doll, Cortachy, Angus, testament, 1665, Comm. Brechin. [NRS]

ROBERTSON, ALEXANDER, schoolmaster in Dunkeld, Perthshire, 1682. [DPD.2.96]

ROBERTSON, ALEXANDER, in Cortachy and Clova, Angus, 1691. [NRS.E69.11.1]

ROBERTSON, ANDREW, in Fearn, Angus, 1691. [NRS.E69.11.1]

ROBERTSON, alias MCCONOCHY, DAVID, in Dunkeld Perthshire, a sasine, 25 June 1604. [NRS.RS48.3.140]

ROBERTSON, DONALD, son of Donald Robertson in Dunkeld, Perthshire, a deed, 1684. [NRS.RD3.60.475]

ROBERTSON, GEORGE, in Kirktoun of Alyth, Perthshire, a charter witness in 1612. [NRS.GD68.1.143]

ROBERTSON, HENRY, from Kincardineshire, a soldier guarding the Scottish Regalia, then in Dunottar Castle besieged by Cromwell's Army from 1651 to 1652.

ROBERTSON, JAMES, born 1687, in Chapelton, Dunnottar, died 9 July 1732. [Glenbervie gravestone, Kincardineshire]

ROBERTSON, JOHN, in Little Derry, Glen Isla, Angus, testament, 1667, Comm. Brechin. [NRS]

ROBERTSON, or NEILSON, LEONARD, in Doull of Clova, Angus, executor of his deceased father Alastair Robertson, a bond, 1670. [NRS.GD16.42.275]

ROBERTSON, LEONARD, in Cortachy and Clova, Angus, 1691. [NRS.E69.11.1]

ROBERTSON, MARGARET, relict of Alexander Stewart of Bonskeid, Perthshire, and her son James Stewart, versus Neill McPherson or Grant in Strathspey, sometime in Moirclach, Strathardle, Perthshire, on 7 November 1629. [NRS.GD132.59]

ROBERTSON, PATRICK, of Leonach, Glenshee, Perthshire, son of the late John Robertson of Clune. 1640s. [NRS.GD132.62]

ROBERTSON, THOMAS, in Dunkeld, Perthshire, a deed, a heritable bond, 17 February 1662. [NRS.RD4.4.683]

ROBERTSON, WILLIAM, graduated from King's College, Aberdeen, in 1660, minister at Laggan from 1667 to 1669, minister at Crathie, Aberdeenshire, in 1669, husband of Isobel Ross, parents of James, Charles, Lilias, and Elizabeth. [F.6.92]

ROBIE, ALEXANDER, a militiaman in Cullow, Cortachy, Angus, 1643. [NRS.GD16.50.17.4]

ROBIE, ALEXANDER, a militiaman in Egie, Cortachy, Angus, 1643. [NRS.GD16.50.17.4]

ROBIE, ALEXANDER, in Lethnott-Lochlee, Angus, 1691. [NRS.E69.11.1]

ROBIE, DAVID, a militiaman in Egie, Cortachy, Angus, 1643. [NRS.GD16.50.17.4]

ROBIE, JAMES, a militiaman in Corssmill, Cortachy, Angus, 1643. [NRS.GD16.50.17.4]

ROBIE, JOHN, in Cortachy and Clova, Angus, 1691. [NRS.E69.11.1]

ROBSON, WILLIAM, a tenant, with his wife, in Badenyon, Glenbuchat, Aberdeenshire, in1696. [PT]

ROCH, JAMES, died 1642. [Fettercairn gravestone, Kincardineshire]

ROCH, JOHN, of Major Burnett's Troop of Dragoons, from Aberdeenshire, was mustered at Stirling on 10 December 1692. [FBL.295]

RODGER, ALEXANDER, in Fearn, Angus, 1691. [NRS.E69.11.1]

RODGER, BEATRIX, only daughter of the late David Rodger, a merchant in Kirriemuir, Angus, wife of Thomas Meems, disposed of land in Kirriemuir to William Skirling, a maltman in Kirriemuir, in 1698, [NRS.GD137.2487]

ROGER, JAMES, in Blairgowrie, Perthshire, in 1691. [Hearth Tax Roll] [NRS.E69.19.1]

ROGER, JAMES, at the Mill of Coull, in the parish of Coull, Aberdeenshire, 1696. [PT]

ROGER, JOHN, a militiaman in Todhall, Lintrathen, Angus, 1643. [NRS.GD16.50.17.4]

RODGER, JOHN, in Bracow, Navar, Angus, testament., 1676, Comm. Brechin. [NRS]

ROGER, PETER (?), in Redie, Airlie, wife Eufan Rollock died 1640. [Airlie gravestone, Angus]

ROGER, WALTER, in Blairgowrie, Perthshire, in 1691. [Hearth Tax Roll] [NRS.E69.19.1]

ROSE, JOHN, of Easter Clune, son of James Rose a minister in Aberdeen, graduated from King's College, Aberdeen, in 1613, minister at Birse, Aberdeenshire, from 1618 until suspended in 1640, reinstated in 1649 'for his royalist principles', readmitted in 1661 but died that year, he married [1] Jean Troup in 1621, and [2] Elizabeth Wood, father of Alexander, Arthur, James, and Marjorie. [F.6.83]

ROSE, JOHN, son of Henry Rose of Larochmoir and his wife Beatrice Skene, minister at Cluny, Aberdeenshire, from 1607 until his death in 1623. [F.6.87]

ROSS, ALEXANDER, in the Mill of Denety, Aboyne, Aberdeenshire, 1667. [AVR]

ROSS, ALEXANDER, of Birsbeg, Birse, Aberdeenshire, 1667. [AVR]

ROSS, FRANCIS, eldest son of Patrick Ross in Formastoun of Aboyne, Aberdeenshire, a disposition of land on 1 March 1697. [NRS.GD305.1.97.212]

ROSS, JAMES, schoolmaster in Moulin, Perthshire, 1649, later in Dunkeld, Perthshire, 1679. [DPD.2.96]

ROSS, JAMES, graduated MA from Marischal College in Aberdeen in 1660, minister at Cluny, Aberdeenshire, from 1671 until 1680s. [F.6.87]

ROSS, JOHN, minister at Braemar, Aberdeenshire, in 1608. [F.6.85]

ROSS, JOHN, minister at Blairgowrie, Perthshire, confirmed receipt of his stipend on 6 November 1627. [NRS.GD190.2.118]

ROSS, ROBERT, in Edzell, Angus, 1691. [NRS.E69.11.1]

ROSS, THOMAS, minister at Aboyne and Glentanar, Aberdeenshire, from 1651 until 1678. [F.6.78]

ROSS, WILLIAM, of the Earl of Airlie's Militia, Angus, 1670. [NRS.GD16.53.39]

ROSS, WILLIAM, in Milton of Tarland, Aberdeenshire, in 1696. [PT]

ROY, ADAM, a tenant, with his wife, in Crofts, Glenbuchat, Aberdeenshire, in 1696. [PT]

ROY, DUNCAN, a tenant, with his wife, in Badenyon, Glenbuchat, Aberdeenshire, in 1696. [PT]

ROY, JOHN, a tenant, with his wife, in Badenyon, Glenbuchat, Aberdeenshire, in 1696. [PT]

SALTER, JANET, in Alyth, Perthshire, in 1691. [Hearth Tax Roll] [NRS.E69.19.1]

SALTER, JOHN, in Alyth, Perthshire, a deed, June 1624. [NRS.GD16.12.91]; renounced his claim to land in the barony of Alyth on 9 May 1624, to Lord James Ogilvy. [NRS.GD16.12.41]

SALTER, PATRICK, in Alyth, Perthshire, a deed, June 1624. [NRS.GD16.12.91]

SANDIMAN, ALEXANDER, in Alyth, Perthshire, in 1691. [Hearth Tax Roll] [NRS.E69.19.1]

SANDEMAN, WILLIAM, in Airlie, Angus, 1691. [NRS.E69.11.1]

SANDERS, ALEXANDER, of Major Burnett's Troop of Dragoons, from Aberdeenshire, was mustered at Stirling on 10 December 1692. [FBL.295]

SANDERS, JAMES, minister at Lintrathen, Angus, and wife Margaret Ogilvie, testament, 1658, Comm. Brechin. [NRS]

SANDERS, WILLIAM, in Blairgowrie, Perthshire, in 1691. [Hearth Tax Roll] [NRS.69.19.1]

SANDERSON, DAVID, reader at the church of Crathie, Aberdeenshire, from 1590 to 1608, was murdered in June 1614. [F.6.92]

SANDERSON, WILIAM, minister at Glenmuick, Aberdeenshire, from 1574 until 1595. [F.6.98]

SANDS, ROBERT, of Major Burnett's Troop of Dragoons, from Aberdeenshire, was mustered at Stirling on 3 December 1697. [FBL.295]

SANGSTER, ARTHUR, from Kincardineshire, a soldier guarding the Scottish Regalia then in Dunottar Castle from Cromwell's Army from 1651-1652. [DR]

SCADE, JOHN, in Old Kincraig, in Tarland, Aberdeenshire, in 1696. [PT]

SCHERRICH, THOMAS, a militiaman in Cortachy, Angus, 1643. [NRS.GD16.50.17.4]

SCHEWAN, JAMES, minister of Navar, Angus, from 1597 until after 1615; relict Margaret Erskine, testament, 1635, Comm. Brechin. [NRS] [F.5.400]

SCOTT, AGNES, daughter of Robert Scott of Benholm, a grant of life rent of Wester Strath in Fettercairn, Kincardineshire, as in her marriage contract with Robert Reid of Balnakettle, a sasSine dated 26 January 1683. [NRS.GD4.199]

SCOTT, JAMES, in Fearn, Angus, 1691. [NRS.E69.11.1]

SCOTT, MALCOLM, of Major Burnett's Troop of Dragoons, from Aberdeenshire, was mustered at Stirling on 3 December 1697. [FBL.295]

SCOTT, MARGARET, in Menmuir, Angus, 1691. [NRS.E69.11.1]

SCOTT, PATRICK, in Fearn, Angus, 1691. [NRS.E69.11.1]

SCOTT, THOMAS, in Cannock, Glen Isla, Angus, husband of Janet Nicoll, testament,1629, Comm. Brechin. [NRS]

SCRYMGEOUR, JOHN, eldest son and heir of the late John Scrymgeourof Kirkton, disposed of the lands of Kirkton of Egglesstradichtie in the Regality of Kirriemuir, to his future wife Maidlane Wedderburn, eldest daughter of Alexander Wedderburn of Kingennie, Angus, on 11 July 1659. [NRS.GD137.91]

SEATON, ALEXANDER, born 1650, graduated MA from Kings College in Aberdeen in 1670, minister at Leochel and Cushnie from 1688 until his death on 6 April 1707. [F.VI.135]

SECTOR, ALEXANDER, a tenant in Coatmoir in the parish of Coull, Aberdeenshire, 1696. [PT]

SETON, GEORGE, graduated from Marischal College, Aberdeen, in 1604, minister of Birse, Aberdeenshire, in 1614. [F.6.82]

SHAND, JOHN, in Bailzie, Lochlee, Angus, testament, 1626, Comm. Brechin. [NRS]

SHAW, ANDREW, and other vagabonds in the neighbourhood of Braemar, Aberdeenshire, were to be apprehended, by order of John Erskine, Earl of Mar, on 8 September 1663. [NRS.GD124.6.97]

SHAW, DUNCAN, chamberlain at Braemar, Aberdeenshire, 11 September 1691. [NRS.GD124.17.71]

SHAW, JAMES, born 1645, died 18 January 1726. [Kildrummy gravestone, Aberdeenshire]

SHEPHERD, ALEXANDER, and his wife Isobel Oliver, in Easter Craigie, Glen Isla, Angus, testament, 1693, Comm. Brechin. [NRS]

SHEPHERD, JAMES, in Blairgowrie, Perthshire, in 1691. [Hearth Tax Roll] [NRS.E69.19.1]

SHEPHERD, JOHN, a militiaman in Lintrathen, Angus, 1643. [NRS.GD16.50.17.4]

SHEPHERD, JOHN, in Airlie, Angus, 1691. [NRS.E69.11.1]

SHIRRELL, THOMAS, in Arntiber, Clova, Angus, testament, 1681, Comm. Brechin. [NRS]

SIM, JOHN, in Menmuir, Angus, 1691. [NRS.E69.11.1]

SIM, JOHN, in Fearn, Angus, 1691. [NRS.E69.11.1]

SIM, ROBERT, in Menmuir, Angus, 1691. [NRS.E69.11.1]

SIME, CATHERINE, in Alyth, Perthshire, in 1691. [Hearth Tax Roll] [NRS.E69.19.1]

SIMER, JAMES, in Fearn, Angus, 1691. [NRS.E69.11.1]

SIMSON, ALEXANDER, in Navar, Angus, 1691. [NRS.E69.11.1]

SYMSON, ALEXANDER, graduated MA from King's College, Aberdeen, 1666, minister of Navar, Angus, from 1670 to his death in 1707, husband of Margaret Carnegie. [F.5.401]

SIMSON, DAVID, in Cortachy and Clova, Angus, 1691. [NRS.E69.11.1]

SIMPSON, GEORGE, of the Earl of Airlie's Militia, Angus, 1670. [NRS.GD16.53.39]

SIMPSON, JOHN, a militiaman in Colziny, Cortachy, Angus, 1643. [NRS.GD16.50.17.4]

SIMPSON, JOHN, of Major Burnett's Troop of Dragoons, from Aberdeenshire, was mustered at Stirling on 10 December 1692. [FBL.295]

SYMSON, M., of the Earl of Airlie's Militia, Angus, 1670. [NRS.GD16.53.39]

SINCLAIR, JOHN, from Kincardineshire, a soldier guarding the Scottish Regalia then in Dunottar Castle from Cromwell's Army from 1651-1652. [DR]

SKENE, ANDREW, MA, minister at Cluny, Aberdeenshire, from 1654 until 1664. [F.6.87]

SKEEN, JOHN, in Edzell, Angus, 1691. [NRS.E69.11.1]

SKINNER, HERCULES, MA, minister of Navar, Angus, from 1658 to 1669. [F.5.401]

SKINNER, ISOBEL, in Little Dunkeld, Perthshire, in 1691. [Hearth Tax Records] [NRS.E69.19.1]

SKINNER, JOHN, from Kincardineshire, a soldier guarding the Scottish Regalia then in Dunottar Castle from Cromwell's Army from 1651-1652. [DR]

SKINNER, LAURENCE, graduated MA from St Andrews in 1603, minister at Dunlappie from 1615 later at Navar, Angus, from 1621 to his death in 1647, husband of (1) Katherine

Thain, parents of Laurence and William, (2) Eupham Cramond, parents of Hercules; testaments, 1627,1650, Comm. Brechin. [F.5.400/419][NRS]

SKINNER, LAURENCE, son of Reverend Laurence Skinner, MA, minister of Navar, Angus, from 1648 to 1650. [F.5.401]

SMALL, JAMES, MA, minister of Cortachy, Angus, from 1679 to 1687. [F.5.280]

SKIRILL, THOMAS, in Cortachy and Clova, Angus, 1691. [NRS.E69.11.1]

SMART, ANDREW, in Ardgeith, Lethnot, Angus, testament, 1684, Comm. Brechin. [NRS]

SMART, ANDREW, in Edzell, Angus, 1691. [NRS.E69.11.1]

SMART, DAVID, in Middle Todd, a militiaman in Lintrathen, Angus, 1643. [NRS.GD16.50.17.4]

SMART, DAVID, in Lintrathen, Angus, 1691. [NRS.E69.11.1]

SMART, DAVID, packman in Lethnot, Angus, testament, 1697, Comm. Brechin. [NRS]

SMART, JAMES, a militiaman in Lintrathen, Angus, 1643. [NRS.GD16.50.17.4]

SMART, JOHN, in Lethnott-Lochlee, Angus, 1691. [NRS.E69.11.1]

SMART, JOHN, in Lintrathen, Angus, 1691. [NRS.E69.11.1]

SMART, THOMAS, in Lethnott-Lochlee, Angus, 1691. [NRS.E69.11.1]

SMART, WILLIAM, in Lethnott-Lochlee, Angus, 1691. [NRS.E69.11.1]

SMYTH, ALEXANDER, in Margie, Edzell, Angus, husband of Isobel Bellie testament, 1620, Comm. St Andrews. [NRS]

SMITH, ALEXANDER, in Menmuir, Angus, 1691. [NRS.E69.11.1]

SMITH, ALEXANDER, in Navar, Angus, 1691. [NRS.E69.11.1]

SMITH, ALEXANDER, in Fearn, Angus, 1691. [NRS.E69.11.1]

SMITH, ANDREW, in Burnside of Alyth, Perthshire, a deed, June 1624. [NRS.GD16.12.91]; renounced his claim to land in the barony of Alyth on 9 May 1624, to Lord James Ogilvy. [NRS.GD16.12.41]

SMITH, HENRY, in Airlie, Angus, 1691. [NRS.E69.11.1]

SMITH, JAMES, eldest son of Andrew Smith in Heughhead of Finzean, Aberdeenshire, was apprenticed to James Blenshall, a weaver in Aberdeen, in 1671. [ACA]

SMITH, JAMES, in Airlie, Angus, 1691. [NRS.E69.11.1]

SMYTH, JAMES, and his wife Barbara Carnegy, in Cloch, Lethnot, Angus, testament, 1637, Comm. Brechin. [NRS]

SMYTH, JOHN, in Middle Todd, a militiaman in Lintrathen, Angus, 1643. [NRS.GD16.50.17.4]

SMYTH, JOHN, a militiaman in Lintrathen, Angus, 1643. [NRS.GD16.50.17.4]

SMITH, JOHN, from Kincardineshire, a soldier guarding the Scottish Regalia then in Dunottar Castle from Cromwell's Army from 1651-1652. [DR]

SMITH, JOHN, schoolmaster in Rattray, Perthshire, 1686. [DPD.2.98]

SMITH, JOHN, died in 1679, husband of Janet Smith. [Airlie gravestone, Angus]

SMITH, JOHN, in Alyth, Perthshire, in 1691. [Hearth Tax Roll] [NRS.E69.19.1]

SMITH, JOHN, a tenant in the parish of Crathie, Aberdeenshire, in 1696. [PT]

SMITH, PATRICK, in Alyth, Perthshire, a deed, June 1624. [NRS.GD16.12.91]

SMITH, PATRICK, born 1621, a hammerman in Baikie, husband of Agnes Long, died on 11 January 1674, their son John Smith, husband of Janet Smith, died on 11 January 1679. [Airlie gravestone, Angus]

SMITH, PATRICK, a smith, with his wife and son Patrick, in Cottarton of Glenbuchat, Aberdeenshire, in 1696. [PT]

SMITH, THOMAS, in Indorraute, Glen Isla, Angus, husband of Agnes Ramsay, testament, 1662, Comm. Brechin. [NRS]

SMYTH, THOMAS, a militiaman in Rottuell, Cortachy, Angus, 1643. [NRS.GD16.50.17.4]

SOMERVILLE, JAMES, of Major Burnett's Troop of Dragoons, from Aberdeenshire, was mustered at Stirling on 3 December 1697. [FBL.295]

SOUTAR, JAMES, in Alyth, Perthshire, in 1691. [Hearth Tax Roll] [NRS.E69.19.1]

SOUTAR, JOHN, in Fynnach, Lethnot, Angus, testament, 1626, Comm. Brechin. [NRS]

SPALDING, ANDREW, of Ashintully, Perthshire, a sasine, 24 March 1604. [NRS.RS48.3.4/5]

SPALDING, ANDREW, in Blacklunan in Glenisla, Angus, 1691. [NRS.E69.11.1]

SPALDING, GEORGE, in Whiteside of Alyth, Perthshire, a sasine, 25 August 1604. [NRS.RS48.3.233]

SPALDING, JOHN, of the Hill of Kirriemuir, Angus, and his spouse Barbara Blair, a transaction re the lands of Inglistoun of Kinnettles, Angus, with Alexander Strachan of Brigtoun and his son Alexander Spalding, a deed subscribed in Forfar on 15 June 1605. [NRS.GD68.1.126]

SPALDING, JOHN, in Drumflogue, Glen Isla, Angus, testaments, 1621, 1628, Comm. Brechin.

SPALDING, THOMAS, in Blacklunan in Glenisla, Angus, 1691. [NRS.E69.11.1]

SPALDING, WILLIAM, a militiaman at Campsie, Lintrathen, Angus, 1643. [NRS.GD16.50.17.4]

SPEED, JOHN, schoolmaster at Loch Lee, Angus, 1690, [SHS.4.2]; in Fearn 1691. [NRS.E69.11.1]

SPEED, WILLIAM, in Navar, Angus, 1691. [NRS.E69.11.1]

STEEL, DAVID, born 1647, in Fornitie, died 1705, husband of Janet Wright. [Lintrathen gravestone]; in Lintrathen, Angus, 1691. [NRS.E69.11.1]

STEEL, JANET, daughter of the late John Steel, in Clova, Angus, testament, 1665, Comm. Brechin. [NRS]

STEILL, JOHN, the younger, and his spouse Margaret Adam, in Westquarter of Alyth, Perthshire, a bond with Lord James Ogilvy in 1629. [NRS.GD16.1.37]

STEPHENSON, JOHN, in Edzell, Angus, 1691. [NRS.E69.11.1]

STEPHENSON, JOHN, in Fearn, Angus, 1691. [NRS.E69.11.1]

STEUART, or DUFF, CHARLES, schoolmaster in Dunkeld, Perthshire, 1690. [DPD.2.97]

STEUART, THOMAS, died on 27 July 1639. [Moulin gravestone, Perthshire]

STEWART, AGNES, relict of James Rose minister at Lintrathen, Angus, 1630. [NRS.GD124.17.623]

STEWART, ALEXANDER, in West Forrest of Alyth, Perthshire, a bond, 29 January 1662. [NRS.RD2.3.923]

STEWART, DAVID, in Edzell, Angus, 1691. [NRS.E69.11.1]

STEWART, JAMES, of Urrard, and Jean Stewart, widow of Colin Campbell late minister of Blair Atholl, Perthshire, a marriage contract dated 1 November 1678. [NRS.GD1.394.21]

STEWART, JAMES, schoolmaster in Moulin, Perthshire, 1679. [DPD.2.98]

STEWART, JAMES, in Cortachy and Clova, Angus, 1691. [NRS.E69.11.1]

STEWART, JAMES, of Urrard, granted a tack of land in the parish of Moulin, Perthshire, to Archibald McBea on 8 December 1692. [NRS.GD1.394.6]

STEWART, JOHN, of Pitfourie, granted Sir Alexander Menzies of that Ilk the lands of Pitfourie and Balnacraig on 12 November 1619. [NRS.GD1.408.20]

STEWART, JOHN, in Edzell, Angus, 1691. [NRS.E69.11.1]

STEWART, JOHN, of Dalguise, Perthshire, a bond with William Taus in Ryear, for 100 merks, dated 7 November 1692. [NRS.GD38.1.396]; he was granted a lease of the Easter Maine of Logerait by Charles Stewart of Ballechan on 6 March 1698. [NRS.GD38.1.154]

STEWART, PATRICK, of Bellachan, Perthshire, steward to the Marquis of Atholl, a Jacobite, who was killed at the Battle of Killiekrankie, Perthshire, in 1689. [APS. Appendix ix.56]

STEWART, ROBERT, reader at the church of Lintrathen, Angus, deeds, from 1574 until 1603. [NRS.GD16.47.16]

STEWART, THOMAS, in Lethnott-Lochlee, Angus, 1691. [NRS.E69.11.1]

STORMONT, JAMES, in Cortachy and Clova, Angus, 1691. [NRS.E69.11.1]

STOT, ALEXANDER, in Menmuir, Angus, 1691. [NRS.E69.11.1]

STOVERT, JOHN, in Cortachy and Clova, Angus, 1691. [NRS.E69.11.1]

STRACHAN, Sir ALEXANDER, of Thorntoun, Kincardineshire, a sasine, 14 July 1625, Nova Scotia. [NRS.RS1.17.342]

STRACHAN, ALEXANDER, graduated from King's College, Aberdeen, in 1651, a schoolmaster in Aberdeen, minister at Birse, Aberdeenshire, from 1663 until his death on 27 October 1664, husband of Jean Baron. [F.6.83]

STRACHAN, ALEXANDER, of Glen Kindle, Kincardineshire, acquired the lands of Murthlie in Kinbethock in May 1642; on 18 December 1654 he disposed of the lands on Kinlywyne in Kilbetho to John McEdward and his spouse Janet Farquharson. [NRS.GD124.1.301/363]

STRACHAN, ALEXANDER, in Newton, a militiaman in Lintrathen, Angus, 1643. [NRS.GD16.50.17.4]

STRACHAN, HUGH, born 1672, son of James Strachan of Thornton, Kincardineshire, a student at the Scots College at Douai in 1693. [RSC.I.62]

STRACHAN, JAMES, of Midstrath, Birse, Aberdeenshire, 1667. [AVR]

STRACHAN, JAMES, Lieutenant of the Earl of Airlie's Militia, Angus, 1670. [NRS.GD16.53.39]

STRACHAN, JANET, relict of John Sibbald of Keir and spouse of Alexander Gardyne of Banchory, Aberdeenshire, a sasine, 1607. [NRS.RS6.3.46]

STRACHAN, JOHN, parson of Kincardine O'Neil, Aberdeenshire, sasines, 1621, 1628. [NRS.RS6.2.13; RS6.3.107]

STRACHAN, JOHN, of Fettercairn, Kincardineshire, a sasine, 1628. [NRS.RS7.3.94]

STRACHAN, JOHN, parson of Strachan, Kincardineshire, a deed in 1698. [NRS.RD4.83.1252]

STRATON, ALEXANDER, from Kincardineshire, a soldier guarding the Scottish Regalia then in Dunottar Castle from Cromwell's Army from 1651-1652. [DR]

STRAITON, Captain CHARLES, was granted the lands of Fettercairn, Kincardineshire, on 4 April 1695. [NRS.SIG.150.26]

STRATON, WILLIAM, of the Earl of Airlie's Militia, Angus, 1670. [NRS.GD16.53.39]

STROWNE, ANDREW JOHN, from Kincardineshire, a soldier guarding the Scottish Regalia then in Dunottar Castle from Cromwell's Army from 1651-1652. [DR]

SUDLIE, DAVID, in Navar, Angus, 1691. [NRS.E69.11.1]

SUMER, MARGARET, a cottar woman in Glenbuchat, Aberdeenshire, in 1696. [PT]

SUMMERS, JOHN, of Major Burnett's Troop of Dragoons, from Aberdeenshire, was mustered at Stirling on 10 December 1692. [FBL.295]

SUTHERLAND, COLIN, of Major Burnett's Troop of Dragoons, from Aberdeenshire, was mustered at Stirling on 10 December 1692. [FBL.295]

SUTHERLAND, HENDRY, a cottar in Balmoral, in the parish of Crathie, Aberdeenshire, in 1696. [PT]

SUTTIE, JAMES, from Kincardineshire, a soldier guarding the Scottish Regalia then in Dunottar Castle from Cromwell's Army from 1651-1652. [DR]

SYME, JOHN, in Middle Todd, a militiaman in Lintrathen, Angus, 1643. [NRS.GD16.50.17.4]

SYMMER, GEORGE, graduated MA from King's College, Aberdeen, in 1604, minister of Fern, Angus, from 1614 until his death in 1653, husband of Jean Arbuthnott, parents of Alexander, Helen, etc. [F.5.396]

SUTER, JOHN, a militiaman in Cotter, Kingoldrum, Angus, 1643. [NRS.GD16.50.17.4]

SUTAR, JOHN, the younger, a militiaman in Lintrathen, Angus, 1643. [NRS.GD16.50.17.4]

SUTOR, JOHN, in Lintrathen, Angus, 1691. [NRS.E69.11.1]

SYMSON, ALEXANDER, graduated MA from King's College, Aberdeen, 1666, minister of Navar, Angus, from 1670 to his death in 1707, husband of Margaret Carnegie. [F.5.401]

TAGGART, JAMES, a cottar in Milton of Glen Muick Aberdeenshire, in 1696. [PT]

TAKEIT, THOMAS, of Major Burnett's Troop of Dragoons, from Aberdeenshire, was mustered at Stirling on 3 December 1697. [FBL.295]

TAUES, JOHN, in Wester Coults, Tarland, Aberdeenshire, in 1696. [PT]

TAYLOUR, JOHN, born 1668, husband of Margaret Blebbar, sometime in Quithill, died on 18 April 1727. [Glenbervie gravestone, Kincardineshire]

TAYLOR, JOHN, in Edzell, Angus, 1691. [NRS.E69.11.1]

TAYLOR, JOHN, in Cortachy and Clova, Angus, 1691. [NRS.E69.11.1]

TAYLOR, JOHN, in Old Kincraig in Tarland, Aberdeenshire, in 1696. [PT]

TAYLOR, PETER, in Easton of Tarland, Aberdeenshire, in 1696. [PT]

TAYLOR, WILLIAM, from Kincardineshire, a soldier guarding the Scottish Regalia then in Dunottar Castle from Cromwell's Army from 1651-1652. [DR]

TESTART, ANNA, servant to Samuel McDougall in Toldor, Glen Muick, Aberdeenshire, in 1696. [PT]

THOM, JOHN, in Airlie, Angus, 1691. [NRS.E69.11.1]

THOMPSON, ANDREW, of Major Burnett's Troop of Dragoons, from Aberdeenshire, was mustered at Stirling on 3 December 1697. [FBL.295]

THOMSON, CHARLES, of the Earl of Airlie's Militia, Angus, 1670. [NRS.GD16.53.39]

THOMSON, JAMES, clerk of the regality of Kildrummy, Aberdeenshire, a warrant, 23 October 1682. [NRS.GD124.17.68]

THOMSON, JAMES, of Arduthie, Kincardineshire, deeds in 1698. [NRS.RD2.81.2.246; RD4.82.129; RD4.83.402]

THOMSON, JOHN, in Edzell, Angus, 1691. [NRS.E69.11.1]

THOMSON, ROBERT, in Lethnott-Lochlee, Angus, 1691. [NRS.E69.11.1]

THOMSON, ROBERT, in Lintrathen, Angus, 1691. [NRS.E69.11.1]

THOMSON, WILLIAM, in Lintrathen, Angus, 1691. [NRS.E69.11.1]

THOW, JOHN, in Lethnott-Lochlee, Angus, 1691. [NRS.E69.11.1]

TOD, GEORGE, from Kincardineshire, a soldier guarding the Scottish Regalia then in Dunottar Castle from Cromwell's Army from 1651-1652. [DR]

TODD, JOHN, in Lethnott-Lochlee, Angus, 1691. [NRS.E69.11.1]

TODD, WILLIAM, in Navar, Angus, 1691. [NRS.E69.11.1]

TRUMPETT, JOHN, of the Earl of Airlie's Militia, Angus, 1670. [NRS.GD16.53.39]

TULLOW, JAMES, the younger, in Meikle Derry, Glen Isla, Angus, husband of Mary Ogilvy, testament, 1621, Comm. Brechin. [NRS]

TURNBULL, THOMAS, in Blairgowrie, Perthshire, in 1691. [Hearth Tax Roll] [NRS.E69.19.1]

TURNER, JOHN, son of John Turner in the Kirktoun of Birse, Aberdeenshire, was apprenticed to Patrick Christie, a merchant in Aberdeen, in 1658. [ACA]

URQUHART, ELIZABETH, relict of David Ogilvie of Clova, Angus, a bond, 1738. [NRS.GD16.19.3]

URQUHART, JAMES, in Alyth, Perthshire, in 1691. [Hearth Tax Roll] [NRS.E69.19.1]

URQUHART, PATRICK, of the Earl of Airlie's Militia, Angus, 1670. [NRS.GD16.53.39]

URQUHART, THOMAS, secretary to the Earl of Aboyne, 1661-1662. [NRS.GD33.63.2]

VALENTINE, ADAM, in Drumhead, Glen Isla, Angus, testament, 1662, Comm. Brechin. [NRS]

VALENTINE, JAMES, a militiaman in Lintrathen, Angus, 1643. [NRS.GD16.50.17.4]

VALENTINE, JOHN, in Lintrathen, Angus, 1691. [NRS.E69.11.1]

VETCH, JAMES, of the Earl of Airlie's Militia, Angus, 1670. [NRS.GD16.53.39]

WAITT, ALEXANDER, in Lethnott-Lochlee, Angus, 1691. [NRS.E69.11.1]

WALKER, ALEXANDER, born 1580, in the Waukmill of Corstons, died 12 ...... 1670, husband of Isobel Burn born 1611, died 17 February 1679. [Edzell gravestone, Angus]

WALKER, ALEXANDER, in Caepo, died on 10 February 16-2 aged 69, husband of Janet Balfour, born 1635, died 14 February 1692. [Edzell gravestone, Angus]

WALKER, DAVID, a militiaman in Dalmartin, Cortachy, Angus, 1643. [NRS.GD16.50.17.4]

WALKER, DAVID, in Edzell, Angus, 1691. [NRS.E69.11.1]

WALKER, JOHN, born 1680, tenant in Jacksbank, died 30 April 1752. [Glenbervie gravestone, Kincardineshire]

WALKER, ROBERT, a merchant in Laurencekirk, Kincardineshire, a deed in 1694. [NRS.RD4.74.69]

WALLACE, ANDREW, did on 16 August 16.... [Airlie gravestone, Angus]

WALLACE, JOHN, a militiaman in Corffie, Lintrathen, Angus, 1643. [NRS.GD16.50.17.4]

WALLACE, JOHN, a militiaman at Purgavie, Lintrathan, Angus, 1643. [NRS.GD16.50.17.4]

WALLACE, JOHN, in Edzell, Angus, 1691. [NRS.E69.11.1]

WALLACE, THOMAS, a militiaman in Corffie, Lintrathen, Angus, 1643. [NRS.GD16.50.17.4]

WALLS, JOHN, in Edzell, Angus, 1691. [NRS.E69.11.1]

WATSON, ELSPET, servant to Robert Milne in Milltown of Glen Buchat, Aberdeenshire, in 1696. [PT]

WATSON, GEORGE, son of Robert Watson of Grange, was educated at Marischal College in Aberdeen from 1635 until 1639, minister at Leochel and Cushnie, Aberdeenshire, from 1651 until 1681, husband of Margaret Forbes. [F.VI.135]

WATSON, ISOBEL, born 1626, wife of John Nicoll, died on 16 March 1695. [Airlie gravestone, Angus]

WATSON, JAMES, in Balntor, a militiaman in Lintrathen, Angus, 1643. [NRS.GD16.50.17.4]

WATT, DAVID, born 1661, resident of Dykehead, died 1741. [Cortachy gravestone, Angus]

WATT, DAVID, in Edzell, Angus, 1691. [NRS.E69.11.1]

WATT, JAMES, in Edzell, Angus, 1691. [NRS.E69.11.1]

WATT, JAMES, in Fearn, Angus, 1691. [NRS.E69.11.1]

WATT, JAMES, and his wife Elspet Ogilvie, in Glen Isla, Angus, testament, 1680, Comm. Brechin. [NRS]

WATT, JOHN, in Kirkton of Glenesk, Angus, testament, 1649, Comm. Brechin. [NRS]

WATT, JOHN, in Edzell, Angus, 1691. [NRS.E69.11.1]

WATT, JOHN, and his wife Margaret Ogilvie, testament, 1693, Comm. Brechin. [NRS]

WATT, PATRICK, in Easton,Tarland, Aberdeenshire, in 1696. [PT]

WATTERSON, ANDREW, in Cortachy and Clova, Angus, 1691. [NRS.E69.11.1]

WEBSTER, ALEXANDER, in Fearn, Angus, 1691. [NRS.E69.11.1]

WEBSTER, ANDREW, sr. and jr., in Fearn, Angus, 1691. [NRS.E69.11.1]

WEBSTER, ANDREW, in Airlie, Angus, 1691. [NRS.E69.11.1]

WEBSTER, DAVID, beadle at the Kirk of Fearn, Angus testament, 1610, Comm. Brechin. [NRS]

WEBSTER, JOHN, a militiaman in Lintrathen, Angus, 1643. [NRS.GD16.50.17.4]

WEBSTER, JOHN, in Cortachy and Clova, Angus, 1691. [NRS.E69.11.1]

WEBSTER, WILLIAM, in Fearn, Angus, 1691. [NRS.E69.11.1]

WEIGHT, JAMES, in Menmuir, Angus, 1691. [NRS.E69.11.1]

WHITE, ALEXANDER, in Cortachy and Clova, Angus, 1691. [NRS.E69.11.1]

WHITE, ELSPET, in Cortachy and Clova, Angus, 1691. [NRS.E69.11.1]

WHITE, GEORGE, in Lintrathen, Angus, 1691. [NRS.E69.11.1]

WHITE, JAMES, sr., and jr., in Cortachy and Clova, Angus, 1691. [NRS.E69.11.1]

WHYTE, DAVID, a militiaman in Fichill, Cortachy, Angus, 1643. [NRS.GD16.50.17.4]

WHYTE, JAMES, a militiaman in Fichill, Cortachy, Angus, 1643. [NRS.GD16.50.17.4]

WHYTE, THOMAS, a militiaman in Englishmaquhen, Cortachy, Angus, 1643. [NRS.GD16.50.17.4]

WHITTON, ALEXANDER, in Cortachy and Clova, Angus, 1691. [NRS.E69.11.1]

WIGHT, DAVID, born 1622, a shoemaker in Brydestoun, died on 14 February 1692, husband of Janet Broun, who died aged 54 on 7 October 16.... [Airlie gravestone, Angus]

WIGHT, JAMES, in Aboyne, Aberdeenshire, 1667. [AVR]

WILD, KATHERINE, in Little Dunkeld, Perthshire, in 1691. [Hearth Tax Records] [NRS.E69.19.1]

WILKIE, ANDREW, a militiaman at Campsie, Lintrathen, Angus, 1643. [NRS.GD16.50.17.4]

WILKIE, GEORGE, in Lintrathen, Angus, 1691. [NRS.E69.11.1]

WILKIE, JOHN, a militiaman in Lintrathen, Angus, 1643. [NRS.GD16.50.17.4]

WILKIE, JOHN, in Newton, a militiaman in Lintrathen, Angus, 1643. [NRS.GD16.50.17.4]

WILKIE, JOHN, in Lintrathen, Angus, 1691. [NRS.E69.11.1]

WILKIE, PATRICK, from Kincardineshire, a soldier guarding the Scottish Regalia then in Dunottar Castle from Cromwell's Army from 1651-1652. [DR]

WILKIE, PATRICK, in Airlie, Angus, 1691. [NRS.E69.11.1]

WILKIE, THOMAS, a militiaman in Cotter, Kingoldrum, Angus, 1643. [NRS.GD16.50.17.4]

WILKIE, THOMAS, a militiaman in Lintrathen, Angus, 1643. [NRS.GD16.50.17.4]

WILKIE, THOMAS, in Lintrathen, Angus, 1691. [NRS.E69.11.1]

WILL, DAVID, in Edzell, Angus, 1691. [NRS.E69.11.1]

WILL, JAMES, in Lethnott-Lochlee, Angus, 1691. [NRS.E69.11.1]

WILSON, JAMES, in Cortachy and Clova, Angus, 1691. [NRS.E69.11.1]

WILSON, JOHN, a militiaman in Kingoldrum, Angus, 1643. [NRS.GD16.50.17.4]

WILSON, THOMAS, a militiaman in Rottell, Cortachy, Angus, 1643. [NRS.GD16.50.17.4]

WILSON, THOMAS, in Cortachy and Clova, Angus, 1691. [NRS.E69.11.1]

WINTER, ALEXANDER, in Cortachy and Clova, Angus, 1691. [NRS.E69.11.1]

WINTER, JAMES, born 1660, died Peathaugh, Glen Isla, Angus, in 1732. [Cortachy gravestone, Angus]

WINTER, JOHN, in Cortachy and Clova, Angus, 1691. [NRS.E69.11.1]

WINTER, JOHN, husband of Katherine Carnegy, in Makindab, Lethnot, Angus, testament, 1597, Comm. Brechin. [NRS]

WINTER, JOHN, in Glen Markie, Angus, husband of Janet Fenton, testament, 1629, Comm. Brechin. [NRS]

WISHART, ALEXANDER, in Edzell, Angus, 1691. [NRS.E69.11.1]

WISHART, JOHN, of Pittarrow, Angus and Jane Douglas, a bond, 1594. [NRS.GD20.4.43]

WISHART, MARGARET, spouse of David Lindsay of Edzell, Angus, a sasine, 1626. [NRS.RS1.19.228]

WISHART, PATRICK, of the Earl of Airlie's Militia, Angus, 1670. [NRS.GD16.53.39]

WISHART, ROBERT, of the Earl of Airlie's Militia, Angus, 1670. [NRS.GD16.53.39]

WISHART, WILLIAM, of Logie, of the Earl of Airlie's Militia, Angus, 1670. [NRS.GD16.53.39]

WOOD, ELIZABETH, daughter of George Wood at the Mill of Marycoulter, Aberdeenshire, a sasine, 1604. [NRS.RS6.2.9]

WOOD, GEORGE, of the Earl of Airlie's Militia, Angus, 1670. [NRS.GD16.53.39]

WOOD, JAMES, of the Earl of Airlie's Militia, Angus, 1670. [NRS.GD16.53.39]

WOOD, JAMES, in Edzell, Angus, 1691. [NRS.E69.11.1]

WRIGHT, ANDREW, born 1542, in Wester Camsie, died 1610, father of John Wright, born 1608, died 1629. [Lintrathen gravestone, Angus]

WRIGHT, ANDREW, born 1575, died in August 1636. [Airlie gravestone, Angus]

WRIGHT, ANDREW, died 16-6, aged 61. [Airlie gravestone, Angus]

WRIGHT, JAMES, a militiaman in Kinloch, Lintrathen, Angus, 1643. [NRS.GD16.50.17.4]

WRIGHT, JOHN, born 1553, died in December 1631, husband of Margaret Trumbel, born 157-, died in December 1633. [Airlie gravestone, Angus]

WRIGHT, JOHN, died 1633, husband of Margaret ....., died 1633. [Airlie gravestone, Angus]

WRIGHT, JOHN, born 1577, tenant in Castleton, Angus, died 1657, husband of Janet Whyte. [Airlie gravestone, Angus]

WRIGHT, WILLIAM, a militiaman at Campsie, Lintrathen, Angus, 1643. [NRS.GD16.50.17.4]

WRIGHT, WILLIAM, in Kildrie in Glenisla, Angus, 1691. [NRS.E69.11.1]

WYLLIE, WILLIAM, son of James Wyllie in Fetteresso, Kincardineshire, was apprenticed to Robert Moir, a dyer in Aberdeen, in 1663. [ACA]

YOUNG, CHARLES, schoolmaster at Tullich, was appointed to collect a list of Pollable persons in Glenmuick, Aberdeenshire in 1696. [PT]

YOUNG, JAMES, in Fearn, Angus, 1691. [NRS.E69.11.1]

YOUNG, JAMES, in Cortachy and Clova, Angus, 1691. [NRS.E69.11.1]

YOUNG, JAMES, in Milton of Clova, Angus, husband of Marjorie Barron, testament, 1658, Comm. Brechin. [NRS]

YOUNG, JOHN, in Blackhaugh, Navar, Angus, husband of Janet Bellie, testament, 1623, Comm. Brechin. [NRS]

YOUNG, JOHN, in Arntibber, Clova, Angus, militiaman in 1643. [NRS.GD16.50.17.4]

YOUNG, JOHN, minister at Birse, Aberdeenshire, from 1651 until deposed in 1660, died 18 October 1671, husband of Elizabeth Ferguson, parents of Alexander, Francis, and three others. [F.6.83]

YOUNG, JOHN, of Major Burnett's Troop of Dragoons, from Aberdeenshire, was mustered at Stirling on 3 December 1697. [FBL.295]

YOUNG, THOMAS, in Blairgowrie, Perthshire, in 1691. [Hearth Tax Roll][NRS.E69.19.1]

REFERENCES

ACA = Aberdeen City Archives

APS = Acts of the Parliament of Scotland

AVR = Aberdeenshire Valuation Roll

BC = Bamff Charters and Papers 1232-1703. [Oxford 1915]

DR = In Defence of the Regalia, 1651-1652, [London, 1910]

DUAS = Dundee University Archival Service

F = Fasti Ecclesiae Scoticanae, [Edinburgh. 1920s-]

FBL = Family of Burnett of Leys, [Aberdeen, 1901]

MCA = Marischal College, Aberdeen

NRS = National Records of Scotland

PT = Poll Tax of 1696

RA = Records of Aboyne, [Aberdeen, 1894]

SHS = Scottish History Society

TNA = The National Archives, London

www.ingramcontent.com/pod-product-compliance
Lightning Source LLC
Chambersburg PA
CBHW051753230426
43670CB00012B/2264